THE
unVALENTINE

STORY BY
SAM BEESON

PAINTINGS BY
JESSE DRAPER

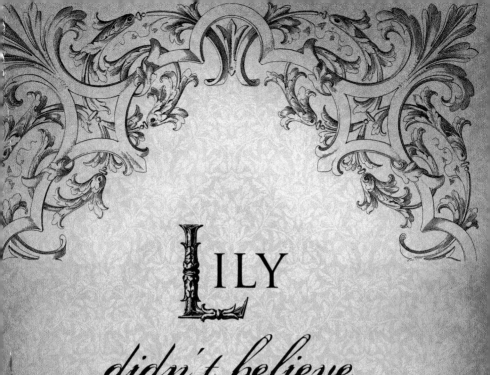

LILY

didn't believe.

To

look at her you'd never guess
that Lily was so sour.

She daily combed her hair
and brushed her teeth
and took a shower.

Her nails were clean,
her cheekbones high
(an icon in her gender),

But these external cutes
did not exactly represent her.

Lily

didn't believe

in love.

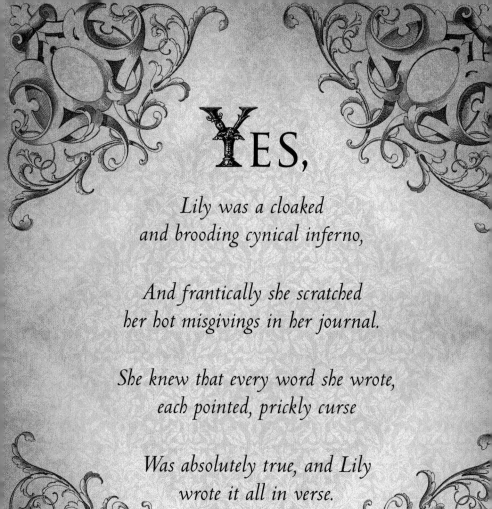

Yes,

Lily was a cloaked
and brooding cynical inferno,

And frantically she scratched
her hot misgivings in her journal.

She knew that every word she wrote,
each pointed, prickly curse

Was absolutely true, and Lily
wrote it all in verse.

LILY

didn't believe,
so she wrote:

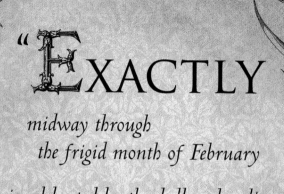

"EXACTLY
midway through
    the frigid month of February

A day is celebrated by the dull and ordinary.

And all around me
    notes are passed by idiots and stupids—

Packed with
    sugar-mottoed hearts and naked, pudgy cupids.

This ritual, conducted under
    heart-shaped, crimson flag,

Does absolutely nothing for me,
    but to make me gag!"

Nope.

Lily didn't believe in love.

Thus

felt the cynic Lily
as she sat and swung her swing,

Alone out on the tarmac, criticizing everything.

She hated love, she hated notes, and being Valentined,

And most of all she hated all the Valentine inclined.

Alone she sat at recess——scritching,
scratching out her scruples.

Alone she sat in class amid
the love-struck, stilted pupils.

LILY

didn't think she *believed in love...*

until ...

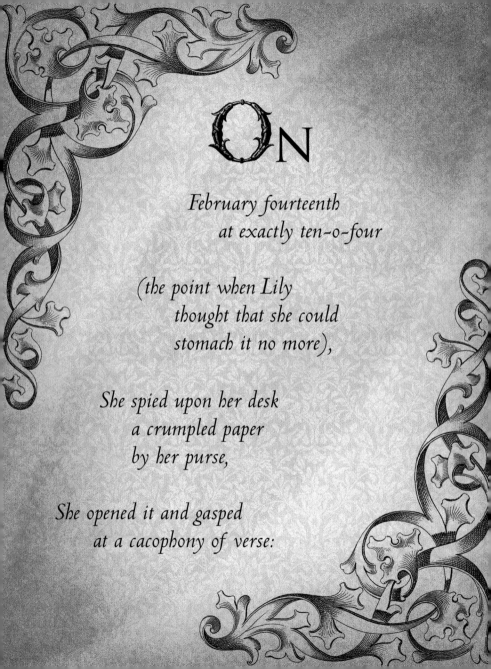

ON

February fourteenth
at exactly ten-o-four

(the point when Lily
thought that she could
stomach it no more),

She spied upon her desk
a crumpled paper
by her purse,

She opened it and gasped
at a cacophony of verse:

"LILY—

I can stand in the rain all day
without shoes.

I don't need no holiday with cupids.

When I want passion, I don't buy
no mango-colored drink.

I want stories——the kind your eyes
tell me
. . . every day
. . . every way.

Ray

p.s. Do you like
black roses?"

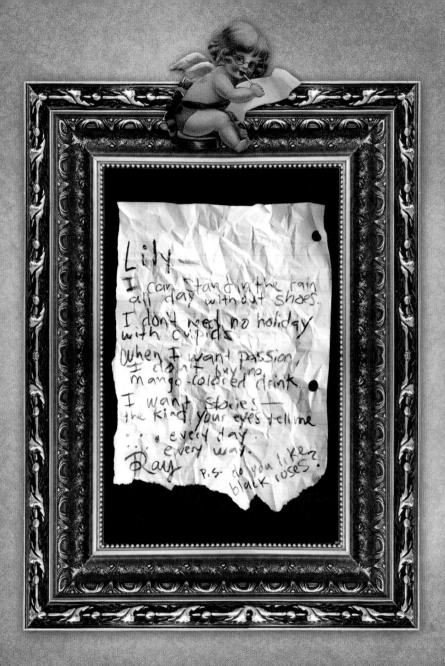

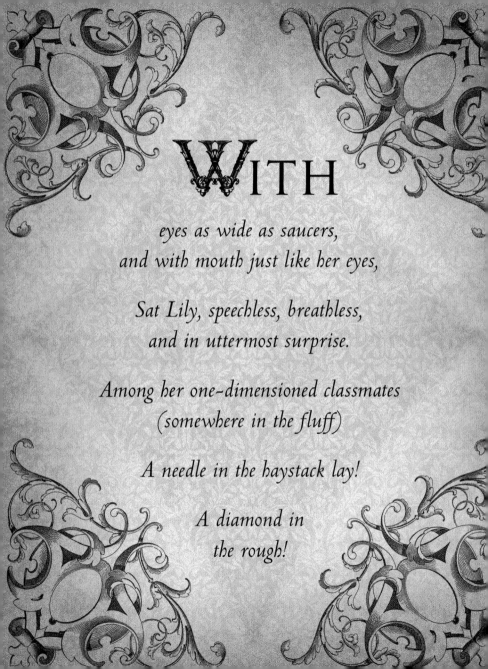

With

eyes as wide as saucers,
and with mouth just like her eyes,

Sat Lily, speechless, breathless,
and in uttermost surprise.

Among her one-dimensioned classmates
(somewhere in the fluff)

A needle in the haystack lay!

A diamond in
the rough!

A
true heart?

THERE!

in the corner . . .

SHE

couldn't understand why thumping heartbeats choked her throat.

She'd never felt a ZING from reading things that others wrote.

SHE
looked at him, he looked at her,
this Ray and Lily pair,

They shared a look and love for
discontent right then, right there.

THE

*day that seemed to smother her
with all things cute and kind*

*Seemed now to coax her hardened heart
to be unValentined.*

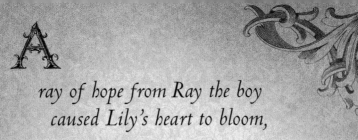

A ray of hope from Ray the boy
caused Lily's heart to bloom,

And Lily's hate for Valentine's
got up and left the room.

THESE

gothic lovers—discontented, passionate, and young—
These rebel lovers ran away, and as they ran, they clung.

If there's a moral to this dark, pathetic little verse,
It lies in finding gold amidst the seemingly perverse.

To those who say that lover's day is ball and chain and fetter
Lily and her Ray agree . . .

And nothing could be better.

To my Valentine

For all passionate, resolved women like my Sarah
—SB

To the loving memory of my grandfather Lee Campbell Knell, my first teacher;
and to my cousin Hal Mark Magleby who drew castles with me
—JD

Text © 2007 Sam Beeson
Illustrations © 2007 Jesse Draper

Visit us at ShadowMountain.com

Beeson, Sam.
  The unvalentine/written by Sam Beeson; illustrated by Jesse Draper.
     p. cm.
  ISBN 978-1-59038-843-3 (hardcover : alk. paper)
  1. Valentine's Day—Poetry. I. Draper, Jesse, ill. II. Title.
PS3602.E367U68 2007
811'.6—dc22   2007032818

Printed in the United States of America

10   9   8   7   6   5   4   3   2   1

SHADOW
MOUNTAIN

Hate Valentine's?

Me too.

Let's kiss!

To:

From:

Chocolate? Nah.

Flowers? No thanks.

Dinner and a movie? Nope.

Commitment? YES!

To:

From:

VALENTINE'S DAY

I must admit
I can't resist,
I wish the day
Did not exist.

To:

From:

Paintings © 2007 Jesse Draper from the book, THE UNVALENTINE. Story told by Sam Beeson and paintings by Jesse Draper.

I trust you, so I confide:
When V-Day comes,
I run and bide.

To:

From:

Paintings © 2007 Jesse Draper from the book, THE UNVALENTINE. Story told by Sam Beeson and paintings by Jesse Draper.

When I want
A box of chocolates,
I buy it . . .
Then I eat it.
All of it.

To:

From:

In the space below,
Write a word
That describes Valentine's Day
And rhymes with Cupid.

_____

To:

From:

SAM BEESON teaches creative writing, Shakespeare, and English at American Fork High School. He and his wife, Sarah, love their five kiddies: enviable Eliza, biddable Buzz, coquettish Claire, jokester Jack, and amazing Andy. Sam tries to write something every day and spends his leisure time ignoring the family dog, Happy, and playing Grammar Punk.

JESSE DRAPER has been drawing, water-coloring, and oil painting since he started cutting teeth. A classically trained artist, he spent years overseas studying Russian icons, collecting unique cameras, and eating lots of cabbage. His north-facing studio gives him just enough privacy to make him happy and just enough indirect lighting to paint images such as those seen in this book.

"Gabriella, are you all right?" Shane asked.

She rubbed her hand over her eyes and nodded.

"Let me help you," he said, gingerly urging her upright. She leaned heavily against him as they continued moving through the woods.

"Maybe we can hide over there," Gabriella murmured.

He turned to the left and saw what she meant. A huge tree had fallen, but instead of hugging the ground, it was propped up at thigh level by the massive branches at the far end.

Not the ideal place to hide, but it might work long enough that he could radio for help. He took Gabriella's hand and silently led the way to the fallen tree.

"Right here," he said, indicating the thickest area of the tree. Gabriella didn't argue, collapsing to the ground and leaning against the rough bark.

Shane stayed right next to her, using his body as a shield as he took a few minutes to sweep his gaze across the area.

There was a part of him that wanted to keep moving, just in case, but at the same time, their backup was so close they only needed to hang on for a little while longer.

He crouched protectively over her and waited, hoping his teammates would arrive soon.

For we are God's handiwork, created in Christ Jesus to do good works, which God prepared in advance for us to do.
—Ephesians 2:10

This book is dedicated to my wonderful niece, Michaela Wanke, who has grown into an awesome young lady. Michaela, always remember you can do anything you want in life as long as you follow your faith and your heart. I love you!

ONE

Dr. Gabriella Fielding walked outside into the starry night, grateful to be leaving the busy ER behind. It took a minute for the chilly September air to penetrate the haze that clouded her mind.

Exhaustion didn't come close to describing how she felt. Every muscle in her body ached, especially the soles of her feet. And the pounding in her temples matched the beat of her heart.

Even her eyelashes hurt.

She'd been up over twenty-four hours straight, running trauma resuscitations and performing surgery for what felt like forever. Summer had given way to fall, but Milwaukee's trauma season wasn't over yet. The injured patients had continued to roll in. This was what she'd trained for, what she was meant to do, healing people who were victims of violence. Yet right now, responsibility weighed heavily on her shoulders, and it was all she could do to make it through one day at a time.

She hadn't eaten since breakfast, but she was too tired to be hungry. Her shift was finally over, should have been over several hours ago, except that the last surgical case had been a two-physician job, requiring her to stay. Her patients always came first, so she hadn't complained. But now she wanted nothing more than to go home and crawl into bed. With any luck she'd be able to sleep for a good twelve hours.

Thankfully, the cold air was helping to wake her up a bit. She only lived a mile away, but decided it might be better to drive home with her windows open, using the cold air to help stay alert.

A brisk north breeze hit her in the face as she left the shelter of the hospital building. She shivered and wrapped the edges of her lab coat together, quickening her pace as she headed across the street toward the concrete parking structure. All she could think about was that every aching step took her closer to home.

Without warning, two men dressed in black appeared out of nowhere. One grabbed her right arm, his fingers biting deep into her flesh, while the other guy roughly clasped her left arm. Terror roiled through her, but her reaction time was sluggish, and by the time she opened her mouth to scream, one of them clamped his hand over her mouth while the other guy rammed what felt like a gun painfully into her side.

"Don't make us kill you," the man with the weapon said in a low, gravelly voice.

She wanted to struggle, to fight, but she was outnumbered and didn't have the strength to fight two big, muscular armed men. Besides, she knew, with far too much detail, how much damage a bullet could do to internal organs.

What did these thugs want with her? Gabby racked her brain, desperately trying to figure out what was going on. She didn't have her purse, but she did have a little cash in her pocket. However, so far they hadn't demanded money…

A huge four-door black truck suddenly came rolling out of the parking structure, stopping right at the curb. The guy with the gun yanked open the door to the backseat.

"Get in," he said.

She began to balk, to search frantically for help, but the man with his hand over her mouth lifted her up as if she weighed nothing, and shoved her inside the vehicle.

Petrified, she attempted to cry out, but only managed to make grunting sounds over the hand he kept plastered over her mouth.

"Shut up," he barked, following her inside. Despite the small space, he crawled over her so the guy with the gun could get in, too. Seconds later, the driver pulled away from the curb, taking her away from the hospital.

Gabby's heart beat frantically in her chest.

Somehow this didn't seem like a random attack. But she still couldn't imagine why she was a target. Unless…they knew she was a surgeon and were taking her somewhere because they needed her help.

Yes! That actually made a crazy sort of sense.

She'd done a house call once before, for the brother of one of the ER nurses. Shane Hawkins had been seriously injured while working undercover and couldn't afford to go to the hospital, knowing that all gunshot wounds were immediately reported to the police. Since he didn't know who within the force she could trust, she'd followed Leah's directions, coming to the remote cabin where Shane was on the verge of succumbing to a serious infection.

Was this a similar case then? Someone driven to extremes because they needed a surgeon's help? Kidnapping at gunpoint seemed a bit drastic, but she'd rather believe that than the alternative.

"Don't hurt her too badly—Creighton wants to talk to her," the driver said in a low voice.

Creighton? Who was Creighton? And why did he want her?

"I know the plan," the man on her right responded in an irritated tone. The guy on her left unexpectedly took his hand away from her mouth and for a second she gasped, filling her lungs with badly needed oxygen.

If she screamed would anyone hear her?

Then her brief moment of relief vanished as he took what appeared like an old rag and jammed it hard against her mouth, forcing her jaws open. She thrashed her head from side to side, trying to evade the gag, but it was no use. He pulled the ends hard enough to cause pain before tying them together behind her head.

The rag tasted and smelled awful, a mixture of oil and gas, and her stomach lurched as she gagged. Feeling desperate, she fought back the urge to throw up, knowing she'd only choke to death on her own vomit. Thankfully her belly was empty.

There had to be some mistake. She didn't know anyone named Creighton! Would they kill her outright if they found out they'd grabbed the wrong person?

"Here, use this," the guy on her left said, holding out a length of rope. Before she could blink, the guy on the right had wrapped the rope tightly around her wrists.

Tears pricked her eyes as the truck took her farther and farther away from the medical center campus. So far, neither man had seemed interested in sexual assault, but maybe that was yet to come? Her gut knotted painfully at the thought. Her past experience with a guy she dated during her residency wasn't reassuring. She'd managed to get away back then, but there were three guys this time around. No way would she beat those odds.

Panic welled in her chest and she had to concentrate on slowing down her breathing through her nose so she didn't pass out. How long before anyone knew she was gone? She wasn't due back at the hospital for the next two days, although she was on secondary call, which meant if trauma cases continued to come in, it was possible she'd be required to assist.

But she was afraid that by the time anyone realized she was missing, it would be too late.

Milwaukee county sheriff's deputy Shane "Hawk" Hawkins was headed toward the ER entrance of Trinity Medical Center when he caught a glimpse of Dr. Gabriella Fielding hurrying along the sidewalk that paralleled the side of the hospital building. She was easily recognizable by her profile, her dainty features etched in his memory, not to mention her long curly red hair and slender frame. Despite the cool September night, she wasn't wearing a jacket but held her white lab coat wrapped tightly around her as if to shield herself against the chill.

Shane scowled. Why on earth was Gabriella walking alone at midnight? Was this normally the time her trauma surgery shift ended? The medical center was located in a relatively safe neighborhood, but she should at least have a security escort taking her to her car.

Gabby had helped Shane six months ago when he'd been injured during an undercover operation. His sister, Leah, had called in a favor, asking Gabby to come to the isolated cabin where he'd been hiding to help out. The pretty trauma surgeon had been younger than he'd expected and had not only skillfully done surgery to remove the bullet from his shoulder, but provided fluids and antibiotics, too.

Gabriella had saved his life.

For which he owed her a huge debt of gratitude.

Shane was supposed to go inside Trinity Medical to obtain the bullet from their most recent shooting victim, but on impulse he quickly changed direction, bypassing the ER entrance to follow Gabby. He'd only seen her once since she'd saved his life, but she'd been busy during a trauma resuscitation and probably hadn't noticed him standing off to the side. This time, he had the chance to actually talk to her.

He was driven by the need to thank her again for what she'd done for him. And, if he were honest, he'd admit that he'd thought of Gabby often over the past few months, even though he wasn't interested in a relationship. Being burned by his former fiancée had taught him that he was better off alone. Linda had mistaken gratitude for love, and had found someone else even while they'd been engaged. A fact he'd discovered six months before the wedding.

He realized afterward that he should have known better. He'd helped Linda get rid of her abusive ex-boyfriend and she'd been the one who'd turned their friendship into something more. He'd fallen for her, but once the danger was over, she eventually discovered she hadn't felt the same way.

Maybe he'd rushed into things because he'd wanted a family. He and Leah had bonded in the years since their mother died. They'd taken care of each other and he'd thought—well it didn't matter. No way was he willing to go down that path of caring about someone again.

Shane would be content being the uncle to Leah's son and any other children she and his buddy Isaac were blessed with.

Besides, would Gabriella even remember him after all this time? She took care of dozens of patients. Was he a fool to try and talk to her?

Probably, but even knowing that wasn't enough to deter him. He'd thank her for saving his life, she'd accept his gratitude, and then they'd smile and go their separate ways.

As Gabriella approached the entryway of the parking structure, two men dressed in black suddenly surrounded her. Shane quickened his pace, watching in horror when a large black pickup truck pulled out of the parking structure in time for the two men to roughly shove Gabby inside.

No! Shane reacted without thinking, sprinting after the truck, keeping in the shadows as much as possible. Thankfully, his black SWAT uniform helped him blend into the night. The driver of the truck wasn't speeding, obviously smart enough to know he shouldn't attract undue attention. As the vehicle slowed at the stop sign, Shane chose that moment to dart out of the shadows and grab on to the edge of the tailgate. He hung there, his muscles tense with the effort, and silently prayed the driver wouldn't notice.

The truck picked up speed and his fingers began to cramp as he clung precariously to the rear end of the truck, bracing his feet awkwardly on the bumper. When the vehicle hit a pothole, the back end bounced wildly, nearly throwing him off. He tightened his grip on the tailgate, determined to stick like glue.

He needed to swing himself up and inside the open bed of the truck, but also couldn't afford to tip off the men who'd kidnapped Gabriella. He was seriously outnumbered. There were at least three of them inside—the two men who'd grabbed her and the driver. But with the tinted windows hiding them from view, he couldn't discount the possibility of a fourth man, who could be sitting in the front passenger seat.

Three to four men for one hostage? Seemed

extreme. They'd obviously come prepared. And why on earth did they want Gabriella?

A red traffic light loomed up ahead and Shane waited for the truck to slow down before making his move. The momentum of the vehicle's deceleration pushed him closer against thee metal frame. Using that to his advantage, he carefully eased one leg over the edge of the tailgate, hoping the driver wasn't looking in his rearview mirror.

The light turned green and the truck picked up speed. He hung there with one leg over the tailgate for a moment, before he was able to push upward with his other foot to get over the edge. He rolled over and landed inside the truck bed with a thud that sounded unbearably loud to his ears.

He froze, his pulse skyrocketing as he hid his face beneath the black sleeve of his arm to avoid being detected. He prayed that the men who'd taken Gabriella wouldn't look back there to find him. Several moments passed before he realized he was safe.

For now.

Shane carefully lifted his head to look around the bed of the truck. There wasn't anything back there from what he could see, so he belly crawled to the front, hugging the top edge directly beneath the rear window. He had to brace himself to avoid being tossed from side to side across the open space like a sack of potatoes. When the truck turned a corner and then accelerated even further, he hung on and peered over the edge, squinting against the harsh wind rushing past while trying to focus on landmarks.

A large sign loomed above him, confirming his suspicions. They were on Highway 45, heading north.

His radio was clipped to his lapel and he knew he needed to call for backup. He should have called immediately, but he'd been determined not to let the truck get away with Gabriella inside. It was a split-second decision he didn't regret.

He pressed himself into the corner of the truck, hoping that no one would see him if they happened to look through the back window. He flipped the switch on his radio, covering the speaker with his hand.

"This is unit twelve," he whispered urgently. "Crime in process, officer in need of assistance."

"You're breaking up, please repeat," the dispatcher said in what seemed to be an excruciatingly loud voice.

Shane winced and continued to hold his hand over the speaker to muffle the noise as much as possible. "Ten thirty-one," he hissed, giving the code again for crime in progress. "Hostage situation. Black four-door truck heading north on Highway 45."

"Ten-four," came the reply.

"No lights or sirens," he added. The last thing

he wanted was for Gabriella to be caught up in some sort of high-speed chase. "Going radio silent."

He shut off the radio, knowing that was against the rules but not willing to jeopardize his precarious position.

Or Gabriella's life.

Shane didn't want to think about what she might be suffering at the hands of her kidnappers. A wave of helplessness washed over him. He had no idea what was going on, or why anyone would take a trauma surgeon hostage from the hospital in the first place. Dragging in a ragged breath, he closed his eyes for a moment, praying the men wouldn't hurt her.

He'd learned to lean on his faith at times like this, and turning to God helped him remain calm.

The truck slowed down, so he peeked over the side in time to catch a glimpse of the exit sign for Highway 60. He frowned, trying to figure out where they were going. There were plenty of wide-open spaces out in this area of Wisconsin. Pike Lake State Park wasn't far from here. Was that where the truck was headed?

Shane had no idea, but he needed some sort of plan for once they arrived at their final destination. And he would have to act fast, using the element of surprise to his advantage.

When the truck picked up speed, he flipped

his radio on again. "This is unit twelve, we're heading west on Highway 60."

"Ten-four," the dispatcher replied. "I have two units responding, no lights or sirens."

"Ten-four." Shane breathed a sigh of relief, knowing that help was on the way. Surely he and Gabriella could hang on long enough for reinforcements to arrive.

But after just a few miles the truck slowed down and turned right again on some sort of dirt road lined with trees. Branches swept across the roof, slapping him around his head and face. The vehicle bounced over the ruts before it slowly came to a stop in a small clearing.

Shane grimly realized that he didn't have time to wait for his backup to arrive. They'd obviously reached their destination and the situation was coming to a head right now.

There was no way he'd let Gabriella down. She'd saved his life and he was determined to do the same.

No matter the risk.

TWO

Gabby was sandwiched between the two men dressed in black, her heart racing with fear.

The only advantage she had at the moment was the fact that they'd tied her wrists together in front of her. Slowly she edged her hands over to the right, trying to reach the pocket of her lab coat without either of the gunmen noticing.

Her wrists hurt from where the rope cut into her skin, but she forced herself to ignore the sharp pain as she slipped her fingers into the deep pocket. She knew she had a scalpel in there from earlier in the evening, when she thought she was going to need it but then hadn't. The one-and-a-half-inch blade wasn't much of a weapon, especially against a gun, but it was better than nothing. Still, she had to get it out of her pocket and take the cover off the sharp edge of the blade before she could even use it.

Gabby could feel the handle of the scalpel, but her fingers were growing numb and she couldn't seem to get a grip on it. Twice she managed to grasp the handle between her fingers, but then when she tried to draw the blade out, dropped it.

Gabby swallowed hard as tears threatened. At twenty-nine years old, she wasn't ready to die, and certainly not like this. What in the world was going on? She led a boring life, one that consisted of working, eating, sleeping and then working some more. Sometimes she read mysteries and tried to get some running in, but not very often. As the youngest trauma surgeon on staff, she was expected to take a good portion of the late-night and weekend shifts.

Her social life was nonexistent, which was the way she liked it. She'd avoided personal relationships since her residency, unable to fully trust that she wouldn't become another victim again. Besides, she didn't need a man interfering with her goal of dedicating her life to helping others.

She couldn't imagine what she'd done to make anyone, especially a guy named Creighton, angry enough to do something like this. The more she thought about it, the more she believed these Neanderthals had grabbed the wrong person. This couldn't possibly be about her. Yet being innocent wasn't going to spare her life. If they didn't rape her, they'd likely kill her.

Sooner than later.

But she wasn't dead yet and just the idea of this being a potential sexual assault made her determined not to give up without a fight. She tried once again to grasp the handle of the scalpel and this time managed to hang on long enough to inch it up into the palm of her hand. Now she needed to figure out how to get the cover off the blade without slicing herself.

Abruptly the driver turned right onto a dirt road and the momentum made her fall against the guy on her left. Somehow she managed to hang on to the scalpel even when the guy harshly shoved her back upright.

"Hope you're ready to cooperate with Creighton," the guy on her left sneered. "Don't bother trying to fight him—he's used to getting what he wants."

Gabby had no idea what that meant, and didn't particularly want to find out. Desperately, she inched the handle of the scalpel farther into her hands until she could feel the edge of the plastic cover shielding the blade.

As the truck came to a stop in a small clearing, she managed to push the cover off the end without hurting herself. She did her best to keep the tip pointed down and hidden beneath the edge of her lab coat.

If either one of these men with guns looked at her hands too closely, they might see her meager weapon.

And then it would be game over.

The thug to her right slid out of the backseat

first and then stood outside and gestured with his gun. "Get out."

Gabby swallowed hard around the gag and scooted awkwardly across the bench seat, trying not to give in to the overwhelming sense of doom.

Despite having worked a twenty-four-hour shift, she needed to stay focused, ready to react at the right moment. The scalpel in her hands wasn't much, but maybe, just maybe she'd catch these guys off guard long enough to run away. She hoped that the Creighton guy they talked about wasn't standing there waiting for her.

The fact that she was wearing a white lab coat wouldn't exactly help her hide for long. White was easy to see in the darkness of the night. Gabby winced. Why hadn't she changed her clothes? It was obviously too late to wallow in regrets now.

"Hurry up," the guy said with impatience.

The truck sat high off the ground, forcing her to jump down awkwardly. She stumbled and staggered off to the side, remaining bent over as she stayed on her feet, hiding the fact that she was still gripping the scalpel.

"Where do you think you're going?" the guy growled, crossing over to where she was standing.

She obviously couldn't answer with the gag in her mouth. There was no one else in the clearing, and the second guy was still making his way out of the car, so when the first guy came closer, she figured it was now or never. His jacket was open and he only wore a thin T-shirt beneath it. Gabby brought her bound hands upward, shoving the tip of the scalpel into his upper abdomen with all the force she could muster. He let out a howl of pain and doubled over, so she immediately turned and ran toward the trees.

Pop! Pop! The sound of gunfire echoed around her like fireworks on the Fourth of July, and she braced herself for searing pain even as she ducked behind the trees.

No pain yet, or maybe she was just too numb to feel it. She kept going, frustrated that she couldn't get out of the lab coat with her hands tied in front of her, and worse, she'd inadvertently dropped the scalpel. Desperately she pushed farther into the woods, not even caring that she probably sounded like an elephant barging through the forest. She purposefully chose the dense areas in an attempt to use the brush for cover.

And while she normally wasn't the type to pray, she found herself doing just that.

Shane crouched in the bed of the truck closest to the passenger side, watching and waiting for the right time to make his move. One guy got out from the backseat first and then told Gabriella to do the same, waving his gun at her in a way that made him clench his teeth in anger. If that guy hurt her… He couldn't bear to finish that thought.

Moving slowly, Shane rose to his feet, plastering himself against the black truck in time to see Gabriella jump down and then stumble off to the side, putting space between herself and the first assailant.

Good job, he thought proudly, willing her to keep her distance if possible.

When the man who'd gotten out of the truck first moved closer to Gabriella, Shane pulled his weapon from his shoulder holster and waited for the second guy to get out, knowing that he'd have a better chance if he took care of both gunmen at the same time.

He was concentrating on the second perp, so he missed what happened. But when the guy closest to Gabriella howled in pain, Shane couldn't help feeling a surge of satisfaction. Using the distraction to his advantage, he turned and fired at the second kidnapper, who'd just gotten out of the truck. When the perp fell backward, Shane turned his attention to the man who was doubled over in pain. He didn't know how badly the guy was hurt, but since he was still on his feet, Shane shot him, before jumping down to the ground. Gabriella was already running into the trees, her white lab coat shining like a beacon as it flapped behind her.

He sprinted after Gabriella as more gunfire erupted from behind him. No doubt the driver, along with the two guys who must not be as injured as he'd thought.

Shane let her run for a bit, knowing they needed to cover a lot of ground, but when she glanced back at him, obviously afraid she was being followed, he understood she assumed he was one of the bad guys.

He caught up, reaching out to grab Gabriella's arm. She swung at him with her bound wrists, her eyes wild.

"It's me, Shane Hawkins," he whispered, hoping she remembered him. "I'm a cop and I'm here to help."

For a moment she stared at him, as if trying to see his face clearly in the dark. His SWAT uniform must have helped reassure her, because suddenly she sagged against him.

He was tempted to hold her reassuringly, but there was no time. Shane gripped her arm and urged her to continue moving. He'd caught a glimpse of the gag around her mouth and her bound wrists, but right now, putting distance between them and the gunmen was more important than freeing her.

Gabriella must have understood because she kept pace alongside him as they made their way farther into the woods. He wove a zigzag path going as fast as he dared, finally stopping behind two trees at what he estimated was a good seventy yards from the clearing.

He holstered his weapon and reached for his knife. "We need to get you out of that lab coat," he murmured.

She nodded, her eyes wide as she held up her bound wrists. He cut through the rope, feeling helpless at the way she winced as blood rushed back into her fingers. He then reached up to untie the gag. She dragged in a harsh breath and it occurred to him that running while being gagged must have been grueling. When Gabriella was finally free, she shucked out of the lab coat, shivering in her thin dark green scrubs.

"Here," Shane whispered. He quickly removed his black jacket and guided her arms into the sleeves. Then he balled up the white lab coat and tucked it deep in the brush. He kicked dirt over it and then straightened. "I'm sorry, but we have to keep moving."

"I know," she whispered back, drawing the edges of his jacket close.

Shane was impressed by Gabriella's determination and fortitude. Her training as a surgeon must be helping her to keep calm in a crisis. Which was a good thing…because they couldn't afford to slow down now. He didn't hear anyone moving through the woods, but that didn't mean the gunmen weren't out there tracking them.

He quickened his stride and urged her to do the same. There was no way he was going to assume the two he'd shot at were too injured to move. His goal had been to wound them enough to get away, not to kill them.

No doubt, the uninjured driver was still out there, searching for them.

Shane turned to the right, hoping they could double back toward Highway 60. His backup should be arriving any time now, but the deputies wouldn't know he and Gabriella were hiding in the woods. And he wanted to warn his team members about the gunmen.

Gabriella stumbled and fell to her knees, breathing hard. His heart ached for her and he dropped down, placing his arm over her shoulders and leaning close. "Gabriella, are you all right?" he asked.

She rubbed her hand over her eyes and nodded.

"Let me help you," he said, gingerly urging her upright. When she was back on her feet, he anchored his arm around her waist. She leaned heavily against him as they continued moving through the woods.

Did he dare use the radio? The last thing he wanted was to broadcast their location to anyone close enough to hear them. Even the slightest sound would travel in the night.

"Maybe we can hide over there," Gabriella murmured.

He turned to the left and saw what she meant. A huge tree had fallen, but instead of hugging the ground, it was propped up at thigh level by the massive branches at the far end.

Not the ideal place to hide, but it might work long enough that he could radio for help. He took Gabriella's hand and silently led the way to the fallen tree.

"Right here," he said, indicating the thickest area of the tree. Gabriella didn't argue, collapsing to the ground and leaning against the rough bark.

Shane stayed right next to her, using his body as a shield as he took a few minutes to sweep his gaze across the area.

The night was eerily silent.

He flipped on his radio and cupped his hands over his mouth and the speaker. "This is unit twelve. What's the status on backup?"

"Two squads have gotten off on Highway 60," the dispatcher informed him. "Please provide your location."

"Roughly two miles west on sixty, there's a dirt road off to the right." Shane wondered belatedly if the deputies had passed them by. The dirt road might not be easy to see.

"Ten-four," the dispatcher responded.

Gabriella looked up and lightly grasped his arm. "Tell them to look for a red fire marker, number 271," she said quietly.

He lifted a brow, wondering how on earth she'd managed to notice that detail, but repeated the information for the dispatcher.

"Ten-four," the dispatcher said.

Shane flipped the radio off and hovered over Gabriella. There was a part of him that wanted to keep moving, just in case, but at the same time, their backup was so close they only needed to hang on for a little while longer.

"Do we have to move?" she whispered, obviously exhausted.

"Not yet, you can rest for now," he replied. He wanted Gabriella to be safe before he could begin to figure out why she'd been kidnapped in the first place.

He crouched protectively over her and waited, hoping his teammates would arrive soon.

Gabby was still wired from the rush of adrenaline, but she wasn't sure her legs would carry her much farther. Shane must think she was a wimp, but he had no way of knowing she'd worked more than twenty-four hours straight.

She was still reeling from the fact that the ruggedly handsome deputy had appeared out of nowhere to help her. Had he witnessed the men kidnapping her from the hospital? No other explanation made sense, and right now she was deeply grateful to know she wasn't alone.

His coat smelled like him, warm and musky. She buried her face in the collar, taking a deep breath. Shane's scent helped to keep her calm as she listened for any indication the gunmen were close.

The minutes ticked by with agonizing slowness. Shane finally flipped his radio back on.

"I need an update," he said in a low, urgent tone.

"Unit ten has been trying to reach you. They've found the truck and three men, all dead."

A chill snaked down her spine and she stared at Shane in horror. "Wh—what? How could all three be dead?" she stammered.

"That doesn't make sense," Shane replied grimly. "I only shot two of them, leaving a third unaccounted for. He was the driver."

"Understood. Unit ten, please confirm the number of dead found at the scene," the dispatcher said.

"Hawk, where are you?" a male voice asked impatiently. "We found the black truck on the dirt road, but we have three dead guys here, and we need to know what's going on."

"I don't know how that's possible," Shane said. "We're obviously not alone out here. Someone must be lurking nearby, and I won't risk exposing the female hostage with me to any more danger."

"Creighton," Gabby whispered, reaching up to grasp his arm. "They were taking me to see a man named Creighton, and told me I'd better co-operate since he's used to getting what he wants."

Shane narrowed his eyes at her. "Do you know this Creighton guy?" he asked.

"No, never heard the name before in my life and I can't even begin to guess if that's his first or last name."

"Subject at large goes by the name of Creighton," he said through the radio. "Spread out and search the woods."

"Ten-four, hold your twenty."

"Are you sure you don't remember someone named Creighton?" Shane pressed. "Someone you work with, one of your patients…or someone from your past?"

"I'm sure." She wasn't about to explain about her eidetic memory. Men tended to look at her oddly once they knew the truth. Yes, she was smart, but mostly because her brain was wired in a way that made it easy to remember things she'd read or learned. But for some reason, men were put off by her level of intelligence. Except for Damon, and he'd turned out to be a horrible brute anyway. She shivered again, forcing the bad memories of the past out of her mind. None of that mattered now.

She felt safe with Shane.

Finally the beam of a flashlight cut through

the darkness. "Hawk? Is that you?" a male voice asked. She could see a tall, sandy-haired man walk toward them, dressed in the same black uniform as Shane's.

"Yeah, we're here," Shane said, relief audible in his tone. "I'm glad to see you, Nate. Are you sure there's no sign of anyone else hiding nearby?"

"I'm sure," Nate's tone was firm. "And when you see the scene back at the truck, you'll be sure, too. Whoever did that is likely long gone."

Gabby's stomach clenched, not that she wasn't used to seeing dead bodies, but generally she preferred to see them in the hospital setting, not where they'd been killed.

"Gabriella, are you able to walk?" Shane asked her. "Or would you rather I carry you?"

"No, thanks. I can walk." She couldn't imagine being carried out of here in Shane's arms... talk about embarrassing! "And please call me Gabby." She dragged herself upright with an effort, secretly relieved when Shane put his arm around her waist again, grateful for his support.

"I'm Deputy Freemont," Nate said, coming up alongside her. She nodded, humbled by the fact that these brave men had put their lives on the line to rescue her.

Especially Shane.

"I don't know how you managed to find me," she murmured to Shane as they approached the clearing. Now that they were walking back to the scene from where she'd managed to escape, she felt nervous, half expecting the men in black to come after her again. "I thought for sure those thugs would hurt or kill me."

"I was supposed to be picking up evidence at the hospital, but when I saw you outside, I decided to head over to talk to you," Shane said. "I just happened to be several yards behind when those two men grabbed you."

"Did you follow the truck?" she asked.

"No, I managed to hitch a ride in the back," he admitted gruffly. "There was no way I was going to let them get away with hurting you."

The stark conviction in his tone sent a shiver of awareness down her spine. Gabby knew Shane was a cop and that protecting people like her was part of his job, but she couldn't help thinking how attractive he was with his dark brown hair and blue eyes. But his big muscular frame was a bit intimidating, even though he didn't give any indication that he'd use his strength against her.

Damon hadn't given her that impression, either.

Trusting men wasn't easy for many reasons. Damon had tried to sexually assault her. And she still resented her stepfather for sending her away at nine years old to live at the Einstein School of Brilliance. He hadn't seemed to care how much he'd hurt her by tearing her away from her mother. And her mother certainly hadn't stood up for Gabby, either.

She shook her head, reminding herself that all of that angst was in the past. She needed to stay focused on the present. Her career. The hospital, the one place she knew she belonged.

She walked alongside Shane and when they approached the clearing, he stopped and placed a restraining hand on her arm. "You shouldn't come any closer, Gabby," he advised. "This might give you nightmares. Stay here with Nate and I'll return shortly."

"No, I want to come," she said, surprising herself with the need to see what had happened.

He frowned and shook his head. "There's no reason for you to have to see this," he insisted.

"Shane, I'm a trauma surgeon," she reminded him. "I've probably seen more gunshot wounds than you."

Shane and Nate exchanged a look of frustration. "I doubt it," Shane said grimly. "Come along, if you insist, but stay close to me."

She was still shaken by what had happened, so sticking close to Shane wasn't a problem. There were several other cops in the clearing, but Gabby's focus was on the dead gunmen.

The closest man lying on the ground was the guy she'd stabbed with her scalpel. Even though she was told they were dead, she found herself kneeling and reaching out to feel for a pulse.

"Don't," Shane said quickly, reaching down to take her hand. "I'm sorry…but I can't risk you accidently contaminating the evidence."

She hadn't thought of this as a crime scene, but of course it was. "Sorry," she murmured. "But you should know this is the one I stabbed with a scalpel."

"A scalpel?" he repeated in surprise. "You normally carry one around with you?"

She flushed and shook her head. "No, but sometimes supplies end up in my pocket. This particular scalpel wasn't the kind we use in the operating rooms but one of the disposable ones that we use to make small incisions as needed while providing patient care in the emergency department."

"I'm really glad you had that with you," he said, looking deep into her eyes. "Using that as a weapon provided the perfect distraction to help me take out the other guy."

She nodded, ridiculously touched by his praise.

"Nate, shine your flashlight on him. There, see? He has two gunshot wounds," Shane said. "I shot at his chest, and can see the entry wound where I hit him. But there's no way I gave him the gunshot wound in his forehead."

"The other two guys have the same type of injury," Nate added, leaning over Shane's shoulder. "They were all taken out with a single gunshot wound to the head. You can see why we figured the shooter was long gone."

"I'm not sure I understand," Gabby said, glancing between the two deputies.

"Dead men don't talk," Shane explained in a somber tone.

She shivered, knowing he was right. Dead men couldn't talk, and she couldn't help wondering if Creighton himself had done this.

And if so, what had he intended to do with her?

THREE

Shane scowled and glanced around the clearing, trying to piece together what exactly had taken place. "Don't you think it's odd that he didn't come after us? Why give up so easily?"

Gabby shook her head and shrugged. "I don't know."

"Did you notice anyone following you before all this happened?" Nate asked her.

"No, but again, I wasn't really paying attention to that kind of thing." She shivered again, and Shane didn't think it was from the cold. "I was focused on getting home."

He wanted to put his arm around her for support, but reminded himself he was here to protect her. Nothing more. "Maybe Creighton heard the gunfire and knew that Gabby escaped with my help. Since he knew I was armed, Creighton decided to kill the guys who had let her get away and decided to wait for a better time to come after her."

"Sounds plausible," Nate agreed.

"But the real question here is why they're after Gabby in the first place," Shane said thoughtfully. "I still find it incredible that they dared to grab her from right outside the hospital."

"I know, and that's been bothering me," she admitted. "Those guys had to be waiting there in the parking structure for a really long time. I ended up working over twenty-four hours straight, and frankly, the only routine thing about my schedule is that it's not routine."

"Is it possible they couldn't find your home address?" Nate asked. "Did you move there recently?"

"Yes, I moved into my current place just three months ago," Gabby replied. "But I only live a mile from the hospital and, considering how everything these days is on the internet, I can't imagine that they couldn't find the address if they really tried."

"True, but maybe they hadn't gotten that far," Nate mused. "Could be that they knew you worked at the hospital so used that as their stakeout point."

Shane knew that with resources, finding Gabriella's address wouldn't take long. "That settles it," he said, taking Gabby's arm and drawing her away from the corpse. "You're not staying at your place alone until we figure out who's after you and why."

"Wait, maybe we're overreacting," she said, backpedaling. "The whole time they had me, I couldn't help thinking they'd grabbed the wrong person. Maybe they mistook me for someone else?"

"You mean they would have kidnapped any beautiful woman with red hair?" Shane echoed drily. "No way, Gabby. This is definitely personal." He gave her a pointed look. "It's obvious they want something specific from you—otherwise, why would they tell you to cooperate with Creighton?"

"None of this makes sense," she said with a scowl. "But I'm telling you, I don't know Creighton and I think they grabbed me by mistake."

Shane turned to Nate, tired of arguing and determined to get Gabby away from here. "Would you mind giving us a lift back to the hospital? That's where I left my car."

"Sure," his friend agreed. "After we're finished here, I'll give you both a ride back."

"Good, that way I can take Gabby someplace safe where this Creighton guy will never find her."

"Wait a minute," Gabby protested. "I can't just disappear! I have patient-care responsibilities."

"She has a point," Nate said. "And really, it might be best if she stays inside the hospital where there are plenty of people surrounding her. These guys waited for her outside because it was a better place to grab her. It wouldn't be so easy to get to her inside the hospital."

Shane hesitated. Nate was right. Being surrounded by dozens of people around the clock was a good way to remain safe. "I wish the hospital security guards carried weapons," he muttered.

"A Taser is a weapon," Nate said mildly. "And I know the senior security guards carry Tasers."

"There are dozens of call rooms," Gabby spoke up. "I can stay in one of them."

Shane considered the fact that Gabby might be safer in a call room at the hospital than in some isolated hotel room. And he could sleep on the floor outside her room as an extra point of security. The floor wouldn't be comfortable, but maybe they could find a blanket or two for him to use as a cushion.

"Uh-oh, we're in trouble now," Nate muttered. "I just saw Griff pull up."

"Who's that?" Gabby asked with a frown.

"Our boss," Shane explained. "He's tough but fair, even if he doesn't know how to smile."

"That guy is seriously intense," Nate added.

Their tall, blond-haired leader climbed out of the police vehicle and strode purposefully toward them. "Hawk, fill me in on what went down," he ordered.

Shane gave him the condensed version and as

he spoke, Griff's serious expression morphed into a dark scowl.

"Why didn't you follow protocol by calling for backup right away?" Griff demanded. "You could have tailed the truck using your squad."

Shane shook his head, deciding this wasn't the time to explain how he owed Gabby for saving his life. "I followed my instincts, and my vehicle was too far away to go back for it."

Griff glared at him for a long moment before he spoke in a grim tone. "Hawk, you're the newest member of my team and a good cop. But I need you to follow the rules. Trust me, if you pull a stunt like this again, I'll cut you loose so fast your head will spin like a top."

"Understood," Shane said, swallowing hard. The last thing he wanted was to lose his job, but he wasn't going to apologize for rescuing Gabby, either.

Given the same set of circumstances, he'd do the same thing again.

"Excuse me, Mr. Griff?" Gabby spoke up.

It hardly seemed possible, but Griff's expression turned even darker. "Vaughn, Lieutenant Vaughn," he corrected in a clipped tone.

"Oh, sorry, Lieutenant. I wanted to make sure you understand how grateful I am for Shane's actions tonight. Maybe he didn't follow protocol but he saved my life."

Shane wanted to tell Gabby to be quiet, that

she was probably only making things worse, but the fact that she spoke up in his defense at all caught him off guard. Was she actually trying to shield him from Griff's anger? The notion was inconceivable.

"Look, Miss—" Griff began, but she swiftly cut him off.

"Doctor," she corrected, adopting the same clipped tone he'd used earlier. "Dr. Gabby Fielding, trauma surgeon."

Griff looked polaxed by Gabby's quick comeback and Shane didn't dare look over at Nate for fear he'd burst out laughing. Obviously, Gabby didn't have red hair for nothing.

"Dr. Fielding, I'm truly glad you're all right, but the end doesn't always justify the means."

Gabby opened her mouth to argue, but Griff shook his head.

"Let's put that aside for now, okay? Have either of these deputies taken your statement yet?" the lieutenant asked, his tone softer than it had been before.

"No, but I'm happy to do that right now if needed," she responded.

Shane wasn't surprised when his boss backed off. After all, Gabby wasn't just any victim— she was a well-respected doctor in the community. She'd been the surgeon on duty after the airport shooting that had taken place ten days ago, and he'd had the opportunity to see her in action since he and Nate had ended up following the victims to the ER.

Watching Gabby in the trauma room had only reminded him how good she was at her job. She was smart, gutsy and never once hesitated doing exactly what needed to be done.

He'd admired her from afar but didn't dare allow his feelings to get personal.

Nate took her statement at Griff's direction. Gabby reported the events she'd suffered in a monotone voice, as if she were reciting a recipe rather than describing the way she'd been victimized. Once again, he was struck by the need to place a reassuring hand on her arm, but of course he didn't. Shane glanced back at the dead men in the clearing. After his dad died, he'd run with a rough crowd and had gotten arrested. He counted his blessings that he'd been able to turn his life around, becoming a cop rather than continuing on a downhill spiral.

"Thank you, Doctor. Are you sure you can't describe the men in more detail?" Griff pressed.

Gabby's control snapped. "I gave you everything I saw and heard in explicit detail. I have a good memory, so trust me when I say there isn't anything more I can tell you." She huffed out a weary breath. "Besides, I've been up well over twenty-four hours straight and I need to get back to the hospital so I can get some sleep."

"We're almost finished here," Nate said.

"No, we *are* finished here. I refuse to be interrogated as if I'm the one who did something wrong."

"Dr. Fielding, I assure you my intent wasn't to treat you like a criminal," Griff said. "But victims often remember more details than they realize. We have to ask questions over and over to get the full story."

"I remember everything crystal clear," she said flatly. "I have an eidetic memory, so there's no point in rehashing this any longer. You know everything I do, so I'd like to leave. Now," she added for emphasis.

"Griff, why don't you let me drive the doctor and Hawk back to Milwaukee," Nate offered. "We can follow up more later if we need to."

"Okay, fine," the lieutenant said with reluctance. "But keep in touch…and Hawk? I expect to see your report on his first thing in the morning."

"Will do," Shane agreed, even though first thing in the morning was only six hours from now. It was already two o'clock and they had a good thirty-minute ride back to the city. Being off duty for the next couple of days was good timing. He'd have a chance to keep a close eye on Gabby.

"Come on, my car is parked out on the road," Nate said as he turned away from the clearing.

Gabby followed the deputy without saying

a word, stumbling a bit as she walked. Shane slipped his arm around her waist, silently offering support.

"Thank you," she murmured, leaning against him. "Do you think we can go to my house to pick up some things before we go to the hospital? I really need a change of clothes."

"If it's safe," he hedged, wishing he could do what she wanted. But he wouldn't sacrifice her safety for clothes.

She swayed as she walked and he told himself that if she stumbled again, he'd lift her up into his arms and carry her, but they managed to make it out to Nate's car without any trouble. He tucked Gabby in the backseat and slid in beside her.

Nate lifted his eyebrow but didn't comment as he went around to take the driver's seat. Gabby fumbled with the seat belt, so he reached over to help her before clicking his own into place.

Shane wasn't surprised when Gabby curled into the corner between the seat and the door and closed her eyes, finally giving in to her exhaustion. He couldn't imagine how she'd held herself together for these last few hours after finishing a grueling shift.

"Is she out?" Nate asked, catching Shane's gaze in the rearview mirror.

"Yeah." He scrubbed his hands over his face, wondering how in the world they'd find this guy, Creighton, before he found her. He didn't buy her theory that she'd been grabbed by mistake. Although, with her eidetic memory, surely she'd remember an unusual name like Creighton.

The more he thought about it, the more he realized that they were better off going straight to Trinity Medical. It could be that the hospital was the last place Creighton would look for her at least in the next day or so.

Gabby shifted in her seat, turning to burrow against him instead of the hard door. He put his arm around her shoulders, holding her close.

"Don't get in over your head, Hawk," Nate warned. "She might be a victim in all this, but we really don't know for sure that she's totally innocent. She might actually know Creighton."

"No way," Shane protested, every instinct in his body refusing to believe the worst. "I saw how frightened she was, Nate. She stabbed the gunman with her scalpel to get away. If she knew Creighton, she would have said something."

"I get that's what you *want* to believe," Nate said bluntly. "But just remember to keep an open mind."

Shane didn't answer, distracted by the citrusy scent lingering in Gabby's hair. He inhaled deeply, letting the fragrance fill his mind.

Yeah, he'd consider all possibilities, but at the same time, he knew he'd absolutely protect Gabby from harm.

Sacrificing his own life, if necessary.

* * *

From the dim recesses of her mind, Gabby could hear someone calling her name.

"Gabby? Come on, Gabby, you have to wake up, we're here at the hospital."

"Sleep," she whispered, pressing her face into the warmth of her pillow.

"Gabby, please, I know how much you need to rest, but you need to show me where your call room is so I can take you there. Then you can sleep."

She heard the words, but it took a few minutes for them to register through the fog in her brain. As much as she wanted to go home, she forced herself to open her eyes and lift her head.

At first she didn't understand that she was still in the backseat of the car, but when she saw Shane so close, she was chagrined to realize his shoulder had been her pillow. "Sorry," she muttered, rubbing her eyes against the burn of fatigue. "Okay, I'm up."

"Good, now just show me where your call room is located, okay?"

Gabby focused on pulling herself together long enough to get out of the car. But the muscles in her body seemed to be moving in slow motion. She lifted the door handle and shoved, barely having the strength to open the door, but then Shane was there with a helping hand.

"Thank you," she whispered. She stumbled out with a low groan.

And then suddenly, she was swept up off her feet and cradled against his chest.

She clung to Shane's broad shoulders as he strode into the hospital through the ER doors. There were several nurses sitting at the triage desk and one of them jumped up when she saw him.

"Oh no, is that Dr. Gabby?" she asked, aghast. "What happened?"

"Nothing happened, she's just tired," Shane retorted. "I need you to show me where the call rooms are located."

Gabby was half listening to the exchange, too tired to be mortified. Just the thought of walking under her own power was overwhelming.

All the adrenaline that had rushed through her bloodstream had drained away, leaving her limp and weak.

"Right this way," the nurse replied. "Are you sure she's not hurt?"

"I'm sure." Shane's tone was firm enough that the nurse didn't argue.

Gabby must have dozed again, because the next thing she knew, she was being set carefully down in a bed.

"Rest now, Gabby," Shane murmured, brushing her hair away from her face in a soothing gesture. "You're safe here. I'll be just outside the door if you need anything."

She wanted to assure him that wasn't necessary, but he flipped the light switch off and left her alone, closing the door behind him.

And this time, she didn't bother to fight against the desperate need to sleep.

"So now what?" Nate asked as Shane closed the door of the call room behind him.

Good question. "I need a favor," he said. "Will you stay here outside her room for a few minutes?"

"Why, where are you going?" Nate asked suspiciously.

Shane had a feeling his buddy wasn't going to like his plan. "I want to head over to Gabby's house," he admitted. "Just to make sure everything is okay."

"So what if it is?" Nate countered. "That doesn't mean Creighton won't show up hours from now, looking for her there."

"I know, but my gut is telling me to check her place out now," he repeated. "Thirty minutes. Give me thirty minutes."

Nate let out a heavy sigh. "Fine, take your half hour. But how are you going to find her house?"

"I'm hoping one of the nurses knows her address," he said. He decided against calling his sister, Leah, because it was the middle of the night and he didn't want to risk waking her son, Ben, or her husband, Isaac, who also happened to be a member of their SWAT team. Since Isaac was off this weekend, Shane knew he wouldn't appreciate being dragged into this mess.

Besides, Gabby's safety was *his* responsibility.

Getting the location of Gabby's home was way too easy. Stacy, the triage nurse who'd showed them to Gabby's call room, had been able to give him everything but the actual house number.

"She lives in the third house from the corner, on the west side of Rivera Street," Stacy said. "It's a brown ranch-style house with tan shutters on the front window. I live in the four-family apartment that's two blocks over and have seen her there several times."

"Thanks," Shane said. "Deputy Nathan Freemont will be waiting here until I return. If you can spare a chair for him, I'd appreciate it."

"Oh, uh, sure, no problem." Stacy frowned. "Is Dr. Gabby in trouble?"

Shane debated how much to tell her. "No, of course she's not in trouble. We just want to be sure she's safe, that's all."

Stacy looked as if she wanted to ask more questions, but he abruptly turned and strode toward the doors leading outside.

After sweeping his gaze around the area to make sure he didn't see anything amiss, he jogged across the street to the surface parking lot where he'd left his sheriff's deputy vehicle.

Following Stacy's directions wasn't difficult and he slowed his speed when he approached Gabby's house. The windows were dark, although there was a small light on over the side-entrance doorway.

Instead of stopping, he drove past, circling the block to park on the next street. Shane silently got out of the car and then walked between the two houses into Gabby's backyard.

There were two young maple trees and he hovered behind the one closest to the side entrance to the house, looking for any signs of an intruder.

If he were Creighton, he'd make Gabby's house his next stop. Shane fully believed the guy was either here himself or had sent yet another flunky to keep an eye on the place.

Shane stayed where he was for what seemed like hours but was probably only fifteen minutes. He was just about to give up so that he could fulfill his thirty-minute promise, when he saw a light flicker inside the house.

His heart thumped heavily in his chest as he carefully pulled his .38 from his shoulder holster. The light had almost instantly vanished, and for several seconds he wondered if he'd imagined the entire thing.

But then he saw the light flicker again, in a

different location, and knew his instincts had been right.

Someone was inside Gabby's house.

This time he didn't hesitate to call for backup and it wasn't because he was worried about Griff being ticked off with him. He wanted the house surrounded as soon as possible.

This time the intruder wasn't going to get away.

After giving the dispatcher the location, he darted from the tree over to the house, plastering himself against the brick. He carefully peeked around the corner to the side entrance.

The light was still on, but from the back of the house he couldn't see the front door. He needed a better position so he could watch both doorways.

The neighbor's yard was his best option. Shane made his way carefully around the neighbor's house, hoping that no one would catch a glimpse of him and yell out, giving away his position. The fact that it was the middle of the night worked in his favor.

After a long three minutes, he was hidden along the front of the neighbor's house, where he could see both doorways. He crouched down to wait.

Almost instantly, the front door opened a crack

and a figure emerged. There was no sign of his backup, but he refused to let this guy get away.

"Stop, police!" he said, stepping out of the shadows.

The figure on the porch lifted a gun and Shane hit the ground mere seconds before the shot echoed and a bullet whizzed over his head.

By the time he looked up, the figure was gone. *No! He was getting away!*

Shane leaped up and dashed over to Gabby's front yard, frantically searching for a sign of the intruder. But he was gone, vanished somewhere into the night.

Leaving Shane to wonder if the guy had found what he was looking for inside Gabby's house? Or not?

He hadn't seen anything in the interloper's hands, but that didn't mean much. But he obviously needed to keep a vigilant watch over Gabby, until he could be absolutely sure she was safe.

FOUR

Gabby woke up, momentarily confused by the darkness. When she figured out she was in a twin-size bed, she surmised she was in a call room rather than at home. She turned over and peered at the tiny alarm clock located on the bedside table. The red numbers read eleven o'clock, but was that morning or night? Without a window for natural light, it was difficult to tell. Especially since she couldn't remember what time it had been when she'd returned to the call room in the first place.

She turned on the lamp located next to the clock and slid out of bed, running a hand through her tangled curls. Her stomach cramped with hunger and her mouth was desert dry, so she headed into the small bathroom.

Fifteen minutes later she felt more human, even though without a blow-dryer she was forced to let her curly red hair air-dry. She checked her pager, to make sure she hadn't missed any calls, before opening the door to leave.

She took one step and tripped over the prone figure of Shane lying on the floor across the doorway.

"Oomph," he grunted as she landed, without much grace, directly on top of him.

"Sorry, sorry," she muttered, shrinking away from him as much as possible as she tried to disentangle herself from his large, muscular frame.

"My fault," Shane assured her, managing to shift her to the side so he could rise to his feet. He offered her a hand up and she struggled to hide her reaction to him. "You look better this morning, Gabby, but how are you feeling?"

"Fine. Hungry," she added as the events from the night before came rushing back. Staring into his mesmerizing blue eyes, she visualized everything with distinct clarity. Had she really allowed Shane to carry her into the hospital like some fairy-tale damsel in distress? What was *wrong* with her? She hadn't gotten to where she was, the youngest trauma surgeon on staff at Trinity Medical Center, by being weak. Her colleagues would never respect her if she continued to allow that sort of behavior to happen.

Time to get back on track. She wasn't the timid, vulnerable girl she'd been as a new resident. Damon had taken advantage of her innocence, but no way would she allow that to happen again.

"Let's grab some breakfast," Shane suggested.

The thought of sharing a meal with the strikingly handsome deputy filled her with a strange sense of panic. "Oh, I'm sure you have work to do, and so do I," she hedged.

"I don't have anything pressing and we need to talk," Shane said, his expression grim. He lowered his voice to a whisper. "Someone broke into your house last night."

"What?" She'd assumed he had been with her the entire time since Nate had driven them back to the hospital. "When? What happened?"

"Let's eat, and then talk," Shane said, placing his hand in the small of her back. "Which way to the cafeteria?"

She didn't appreciate his evasiveness, but she was too hungry at the moment to argue with him. "Follow me," Gabby said, heading down the corridor and then taking a series of turns. She knew all the shortcuts and took a back staircase that came out right near the cafeteria.

The place was busy since it was eleven-thirty in the morning and the lunch crowd was already packed in. She longed for breakfast, her favorite meal of the day, but the hospital cafeteria stopped serving bacon and eggs by nine-thirty, so she settled for a grilled-chicken sandwich and a salad.

Shane ordered a roast beef sandwich and then followed her to the checkout line. He pulled out his wallet, but she waved him away. "I'll put this on my ID badge," she murmured.

"No, I'm paying," Shane said in a clipped tone. He pinned the cashier with a stern look and of course the woman was happy to accept his cash.

Gabby grimaced, belatedly realizing she must have offended his pride, although that certainly hadn't been her intention. In the world of medicine, she was accustomed to colleagues paying for each other regardless of gender.

Besides, she didn't want to give Shane the impression that this was personal.

"Thanks," she said when they carried their trays to one of the few empty tables in the back of the room. "I really appreciate it."

Shane gave a curt nod, glancing around as if looking for somewhere more private. Unfortunately, there weren't many open spaces, much less anything offering privacy.

They took their seats and Shane closed his eyes and bowed his head for a moment before he picked up his roast beef. She was a little surprised by his quick prayer but didn't say anything as she dug into her salad with gusto. Neither one of them spoke as they concentrated on their food.

Once her stomach was full, she eased back in her seat, feeling like her old self. Amazing what sleep and food could do. She pushed her empty plate aside, grimacing when she realized that she'd finished her chicken sandwich and her salad, while Shane was still eating his roast beef. Working in health care, she tended to eat at warp speed in case she was interrupted by a trauma call.

"Did you come up for air?" Shane asked, flashing a wry grin. His smile transformed his rugged features and it occurred to her that this was the first time she'd seen him smile.

"Probably not," she admitted, hoping her fair skin didn't betray her embarrassment. "I've learned to eat fast or skip meals."

"I understand—trust me, it's the same thing for us. Seems that the minute we sit down to eat, we get called out for one thing or another."

She nodded, pushed her empty tray aside and leaned forward. "Okay, so tell me what happened last night," she said in a hushed voice. "How do you know my house was broken into?"

"I was there," he said, his expression turning serious. "But I'd rather not talk here, it's too crowded. Give me a few minutes to finish up and then we'll head over to your place. I need to know what, if anything, is missing."

Patience wasn't one of her strengths, but Gabby nodded and tried not to tap her fingers restlessly on the table while he finished eating. The thought of someone going through her personal things bothered her deeply.

Had he stayed here at the hospital all night because of the break-in at her home? She was oddly touched that Shane had felt it necessary to sleep on the floor in front of her room. She couldn't imagine what the staff had thought about that. He couldn't have been very comfortable, and she hoped he wasn't putting his job in jeopardy by spending so much time with her. After all, his boss, Lieutenant Vaughn, hadn't seemed too happy with Shane last night.

"Do you want anything else?" he asked, rising to his feet.

"No, I'm fine, thanks."

He took her tray and stacked it on top of his before making his way over to the conveyor belt near the exit.

"I'm parked in the structure," he said as she led the way back to the ER.

"Me, too," she admitted. "I'll meet you at my place."

"No, we'll drive together," Shane said, an underlying edge of steel lacing his tone. "You can't stay there, Gabby."

She had to tamp down a flash of temper. Of course she knew that staying at her house wasn't an option. "Thanks, I appreciate your advice."

"This isn't advice, it's nonnegotiable," Shane said bluntly as he held the door open for her.

She scowled but then ducked her head as they walked into the bright, blinding sunlight. She paused and blinked, giving her eyes a chance to adjust.

Shane waited at her side, keeping pace as she began to walk. As they approached the parking structure, she remembered that her car keys, cell phone and driver's license had been in the pocket of her lab coat, which was buried in the dirt and leaves somewhere in the middle of the woods. With a sigh, she acknowledged she couldn't drive her car right now, even if she wanted to.

"This way," he said, lightly touching her arm to steer her to the right.

The deputy-issue vehicle wasn't exactly inconspicuous, and as they approached the car, she winced when one of her colleagues strode past them, acknowledging her with a brief yet curious nod.

Personal news tended to ripple through the hospital grapevine at an alarming rate, and back when things had exploded between her and Damon, it seemed as if everyone had looked at her differently. In the years since, she'd tried to fade into the background, unwilling to jeopardize what she'd worked so hard to achieve. Healing patients was her calling. Her mission. Her life.

Shane, with his dark brown hair, broad shoulders and strong jaw, was far too big, muscular and attractive for her peace of mind. The sooner she figured out what Creighton wanted, or who he was really after, the better.

Because Deputy Shane Hawkins was a dangerous distraction she couldn't afford.

Shane hoped that once Gabby saw the mess left behind in her home, she'd realize that she couldn't stay there. He'd been forced to bite his tongue several times in the face of her stubbornness.

Yet, oddly enough, he was glad her feistiness had returned. He'd enjoyed the way she'd curled up beside him in the back of Nate's car, and carrying her into the hospital hadn't exactly been a hardship. But he liked how she stood up for herself and imagined that she'd had to do that often in her role as a trauma surgeon.

Shane pulled the passenger door open and waited as she slid into the seat. After shutting the door behind her, he rounded the car to climb in. Gabby didn't say anything but twisted her hands in her lap as he backed up the vehicle and left the parking structure.

Once they were out on the road, she broke the tense silence. "Tell me what happened."

He nodded, knowing she deserved the truth. "I went to your house after you fell asleep in the call room."

"How did you know my address?" she asked.

"The nurse at the triage desk told me, which, by the way, isn't good. I appreciate that I'm a cop so she no doubt felt I was trustworthy, but your coworkers shouldn't be sharing your personal information with anyone else, and it's better if you don't confide in them, too."

"I didn't," she protested. "You must have talked to Stacy Mueller—she lives close by and I've seen her around the neighborhood."

"Yeah, Stacy." Shane made a mental note to talk to the triage nurse again, to reinforce the need to keep Gabby's information private. "Anyway, I went over to watch your place for a bit and saw a flicker of light inside. I made my way over to the neighbor's house so I could keep an eye on your front and back doors. Sure enough, a tall guy dressed in black came out the front door. When I confronted him and identified myself as a cop, he took a shot at me and then ran off."

"He *shot* at you?" Gabby asked, her voice rising in alarm. She reached out and lightly grasped his arm. "Were you hit? Are you all right?"

Once again, he was touched by her concern. He reminded himself that her worry over an injury wasn't personal, she clearly took patient care very seriously. After all, she'd taken the risk of driving out to an isolated cabin to remove a bullet lodged in his shoulder. The IV antibiotics and fluids she'd given him had certainly saved his life. He wanted to believe the earnest determination in her eyes was only for him, but more likely the way she was with all her patients.

He needed to remember that she was someone he was trying to protect. Getting emotionally involved would only backfire, in a big way.

"I'm fine, but his shot was close enough that I hit the ground, which gave him the time he needed to get away. And since he had been wearing gloves, we don't expect to get any fingerprints."

"I can't believe this," she moaned. "What is going on? Why is this happening?"

He had the same questions, so he glanced over at her. "Are you sure you don't know what this is all about?" he asked, trying to keep his tone nonthreatening. "You must have some idea what this guy wants from you."

"I don't," Gabby insisted, clearly exasperated. "Why would I put my career, or more important, my life, on the line? This is crazy, my only hobbies are reading mysteries and running, my career is too demanding for anything more."

Shane pulled into her driveway, letting the car idle as he turned in his seat to face her. "Gabby, listen, I can protect you if you tell me the truth," he said in a gruff tone. "But if you lie to me and the truth comes out later, there won't be anything I can do to help you."

Gabby lifted her wide green eyes to his and he could clearly see the anguish reflected there. "I promise you that I have no idea what's going on."

Shane desperately wanted to believe her. "What about old boyfriends or maybe a former fiancé?" he pressed. "Surely you must have made some enemies over the past ten years."

Gabby slowly shook her head. "I've spent the last decade completing medical school, finishing my residency and proving myself a capable trauma surgeon." She hesitated, then continued, "There was one boyfriend during my residency, and I did break things off, but I can't imagine he cares about that now all these years later."

"You don't know that for certain," Shane said brusquely. "Anyone else?"

"Well, there were a couple of residents in the past ten years who resented me, basically making my life miserable, but I highly doubt either one of them is still holding a grudge."

"Why don't you give me their names anyway," Shane said. "Including the guy you dated. It wouldn't hurt to touch base with them."

Gabby pressed her lips together in a frown. "It's ridiculous to think they're involved," she reiterated.

"Then what's the harm in doing a background check, and validating where all three of these guys were last night so we can cross them off the list?" There was a long pause before she conceded. "Fine. The man I dated briefly was Damon Keller—I have no clue where he is now. Eric Ambrose was the resident who resented me the most. I was chosen to be the chief resident over him and he did not take it well. But I heard he relocated to the East Coast somewhere." She released a sharp breath, then continued, "Joe Chasco was another resident who didn't appreciate the fact that I was given the position, either, and he and Eric made my life extremely difficult. Joe relocated to Chicago, I believe."

Shane wrote the names down, intending to follow up on both of those guys. "Chicago isn't that far away," he said as he scribbled in his notebook. "Any other residents who resented you?"

"No, those two were by far the worst."

He tucked the notebook back in his pocket, wondering at the adversity Gabby must have faced during her career. Was it always like this for female surgeons? Or had she been a target because of her genius IQ?

He could see why some of the physicians she worked with might be intimidated by her eidetic memory, but weren't they all supersmart? So why pick on Gabby? His mouth hardened into a tight line. He didn't like the thought of people, especially men, treating her badly.

Shane pulled himself up short, reminding himself that his interest in Gabby wasn't personal. He wasn't about to risk opening himself up for another misguided relationship. Besides, Gabby was clearly not interested in him that way, either. He'd noticed the way she shrank away when she'd tripped over him at the door to the call room. And not once had she flirted even the littlest bit.

He needed to keep his distance from Gabby.

Once they figured out who this creep was and arrested him, they'd both go their separate ways. Leaving mutual respect and friendship remaining between them.

Her house didn't look any different, Gabby noted as she slid out of Shane's vehicle and headed for the garage. "I have a spare key," she said over her shoulder when he joined her.

"That's good, because the lock on your front door was broken by the intruder, so we nailed it shut."

Hearing that made her nervous, but she kept her chin steady as she punched a code into the keypad mounted on her garage. When the door opened, she ducked inside and found her spare key. Then she headed over to the door along the side of her house.

"He left a mess," he warned as she unlocked and pushed the door open. Full of apprehension, she crossed the threshold.

Gabby thought she was prepared for what she'd find, but as it turned out, she wasn't. The kitchen was a mess, although it didn't look as if anything was broken, but each drawer and cabinet was open and had obviously been thoroughly searched.

"Your office is the worst," Shane said his hand resting on the small of her back.

"I didn't expect to feel so violated," she murmured as they made their way through the living room, which wasn't too badly messed up, to the hallway where the bedrooms were located, one of which she'd turned into an office.

She gasped when she saw the chaos on her normally neat desk. "What in the world was he looking for?" she asked helplessly.

"I don't know," Shane admitted. "I didn't see him carrying anything out, but that doesn't mean he didn't have something tucked away."

For a moment panic gripped her by the throat and she bolted past Shane to head over to the bedroom. Dropping to her knees, she pulled out a small cedar box, roughly six inches by six inches wide and three inches deep. Her heart thudded loudly in her chest as she gingerly lifted the cover.

She let out a whoosh of relief when she surveyed the contents. "It's all here," she said, moving the precious items around to make sure she wasn't missing something. "He didn't take it."

"What's in there?" Shane asked, kneeling beside her.

She shrugged, not willing to go too much into depth. "Personal mementos, that's all. Nothing of monetary value. Costume jewelry, like this charm bracelet that my father gave to my mother before he died, photographs of us together as a family. The necklace Leo, my godfather, gave me. Just sentimental things…"

Shane peered over her shoulder and tapped the picture on top where she stood proudly in front of her parents, who were grinning widely for the camera. "You look adorable in that dress," he said, his breath tickling her ear.

His compliment made her flush, and she quickly replaced the cover of the cedar box, knowing that looking at the old photographs might bring back the crippling headaches that she'd suffered throughout her childhood. "Thanks," she whispered, scooting away from him, "but this isn't important right now. I'd better go through my office."

"Sure thing." Shane stood back and let her pass. She carried the cedar box with her, setting it aside. Then glanced around at the mess, wondering where to begin.

"If you're able to tell me what's missing, that would help," he said.

"Lucky for you, I'm extremely organized," Gabby said, gathering papers together. She collated her medical school stuff first, and then the paperwork she'd saved from her residency. She took her time with those, wondering if it was at all possible that Damon Keller, Eric Ambrose or Joe Chasco could have done this.

Gabby bit her lip. Sure, there was a time when Damon might have worried she'd report his attempted rape to the police, but the statute of limitations on that had passed by now. As for the other two medical residents? She'd kept notes about some of the things they'd done to her, mostly trying to set her up for failure. It made her angry all over again to remember the stupid things they'd done—omitting information, or giving her wrong information, which could have caused harm to their patients if she hadn't been supervigilant.

But those shenanigans had happened years ago, and her notes were in a safe-deposit box at the bank. No reason to think that either one of the physicians she'd trained with had decided to come searching for her notes now. Unless they'd been worried that she'd blackmail them? Ridiculous. There was no point.

Still, the idea nagged at her as she continued putting things away.

She worked in silence as the minutes slowly ticked by. Shane helped by giving her stacks of papers he'd taken from the floor and she gathered them together in their proper files.

But as the mess was cleared, she realized there were some papers missing.

"That's odd," she said, poking through the paperwork.

"What?" Shane asked, crossing over to her side.

"So far, the only thing missing is the file for my stepfather's mortgage."

"Your stepfather?" he echoed with a frown. "Why would you have that?"

She sighed, wishing she didn't have to let Shane know all the details about her dysfunctional family. "My mother passed away two years ago and I promised her that I'd continue paying the mortgage so my stepdad wouldn't have to move."

Shane's steady gaze saw far too much. "I take it you don't get along with him?"

Wasn't that the understatement of the year? "Not particularly," she admitted. But this wasn't the time to get into the reasons she resented her stepfather. "But that doesn't matter. Why would anyone take his mortgage file?"

"To get his address," Shane said grimly. "We'd better head over there, just to make sure he's okay."

Gabby nodded in agreement, even though the thought of seeing Richard again filled her with dread. She hadn't seen him since her mother's funeral, and the heated words he'd shouted at her, blaming her for her mother's death, still reverberated in her mind.

Shane didn't waste any time hustling her back out to his car. As he backed out of her driveway, she gave directions. "Richard's last name is Strawn and he lives in Brookmont, so head west on Wisconsin Avenue."

"I know the Brookmont area," Shane said, sending her a sideways glance. "Lots of big fancy houses there."

Yeah, she was well aware of how expensive the property was in Brookmont, but she didn't say anything as he navigated the streets. About ten minutes later, they arrived at Richard Strawn's home.

"Maybe you should wait in the car," he said as he shut off the engine.

"No way," Gabby protested. "I'm coming with you."

Nodding tersely, Shane slid out from behind the wheel and came around to her side. She followed him up to the front door, flanked on either side by marble pillars. She could tell Shane was comparing this huge place with the modest house she lived in, but she wasn't about to explain further. She lifted her hand to knock, surprised when the door swung open.

"Stay back," Shane ordered, going into cop mode as he pulled his weapon from his holster and used his radio to call for backup. "Wait for me in the car."

She ignored him, but grabbed his biceps with

a tight grip. "No, Richard might need medical care."

Shane shot her a fierce glare but didn't argue as he stepped inside the house. "Mr. Strawn? Are you here? This is Deputy Hawkins from the sheriff's department."

Gabby hugged Shane's back as he carefully made his way through the foyer into the open-concept kitchen and living room. Ironically, the interior of Richard's house seemed immaculately clean, not at all messed up the way hers was.

But then they rounded the corner and she saw him—her stepfather—lying prone on the floor, a pool of blood seeping into the cream-colored carpeting beneath his head.

Her stomach clenched as she realized that Creighton had not only come after her but Richard as well. She rushed forward, feeling frantically for a pulse, knowing that if he died, it would be all her fault.

FIVE

Shane used his radio to call for an ambulance as he searched the rest of the house, making sure no one was hiding. He found that Richard Strawn's office was messed up the same way Gabby's had been and wondered if this time the intruder had found what he was looking for.

Once he was assured that whoever did this was long gone, he returned to help Gabby.

"What can I do?" Shane asked, kneeling beside her.

"He has a pulse but it's weak," she said, anguish reflected in her eyes. "This is my fault. He was injured because of me."

"Gabby, listen," he said in a terse, urgent tone. "This is Creighton's fault, not yours. You and Richard are both innocent victims in this."

She shook her head but didn't say anything more. She leaned over to peer at Richard's pupils. "His pupils aren't equal in size—he has a head injury. I want him to go to Trinity Medical so I can keep a close eye on him. He needs to have the best neurosurgical care possible."

"I understand," he agreed. "The ambulance should be here any minute." He put a reassuring hand on her shoulder. "Gabby, whoever did this searched Richard's office. Just like yours was searched."

She paled. "I wish I knew what he was looking for."

He wanted to believe she didn't know what was going on, but Nate's suspicions echoed in the back of his mind. When the shrill wail of sirens shattered the silence, Shane rose to his feet and headed outside to meet his teammates and the ambulance crew.

Nate jumped out of the first vehicle on the scene and crossed over to meet Shane. "I told you that woman was trouble," he said with a wry grin.

Shane narrowed his gaze, not the least bit amused. "The guy who searched her house took the information on her stepfather, which is why we came here. But the perp beat us to it. Strawn is unconscious. From the location of the body, I believe he caught the intruder off guard, so the guy knocked Strawn out and then searched his office."

Nate whistled between his teeth. "What is this guy after?"

"I wish I knew. Could be that he's found whatever he was looking for. But nevertheless we need to convince Griff to put more resources into investigating these crimes." Shane blew out a heavy breath. "We can start with doing simple background checks on the people in Gabby's past. She mentioned an old boyfriend and a couple of residents who resented her, so that's one avenue to explore. And after this latest attack, we need to dig a little deeper into her stepfather's background, as well. It could be that he's the one Creighton wanted all along."

Nate lifted his eyebrows in surprise and then nodded thoughtfully. "That's a good point. And it would explain why her assailants didn't try to kill Gabby last night. Maybe the kidnapping attempt was nothing more than a way to get at her stepfather. And if that's true, then she's no longer in danger."

Shane scowled, not believing that for a second. "Maybe, maybe not."

"You're letting that woman get into your head," Nate accused.

"No, I'm not," he denied swiftly. "I just want her to be safe." He didn't add that he was determined to protect Gabby until he was convinced the threat was over.

The ambulance pulled up, so he left Nate to meet up with the emergency medical techs. He showed them the way to where Gabby waited with her stepfather.

Inside the living room, Gabby gave the two EMTs a quick update of her stepfather's medical history, and then stepped back so they could bundle Richard onto the gurney.

"Shane, I need to borrow your cell," she said. "I have to call the hospital."

He pulled out his phone, punched in the password and then handed it over. Gabby made her call, requesting to be connected to someone by the name of Dr. William Mullen.

"Bill? It's Gabby," she said in a husky tone. "I need your help."

Shane ignored the flash of jealousy, knowing he was being ridiculous, and left the room to give her some privacy. He walked back into Strawn's office. The old man's files had been ransacked with the same thoroughness that Gabby's had. The crime scene techs hadn't found any fingerprints at Gabby's house, so he doubted they'd find any here, but they had to try. Without touching anything, he bent over and read through the papers on top of the desk, frowning when he noticed they were bank statements. And from what he could see, it appeared Richard Strawn was having some financial difficulties.

If not for Gabby's paying her stepfather's mortgage, he'd be living out on the street. He stared at the documentation, wondering if Richard had lost his money as a result of poor decision making?

Or from something illegal?

Maybe Nate's theory was right, that Richard Strawn was the real target. Creighton may have been attempting to use Gabby as a way to get to her stepfather.

Gabby disconnected her call, somewhat reassured that Bill would be waiting at Trinity Medical Center for Richard to arrive.

If anyone could save her stepfather, it was world-renowned neurosurgeon Bill Mullen. Richard would be in good hands, but a heavy dose of guilt still gnawed at her.

Gabby closed her eyes and pinched the bridge of her nose, trying to soothe the pounding in her head. She'd purposefully used her career to avoid her stepfather, mostly because she hadn't been able to forgive him for sending her to boarding school on her ninth birthday. Oh, he claimed it was for her own good, to allow her keen intelligence to flourish, but she knew the real truth.

Richard had wanted her mother all to himself.

And her mother hadn't seemed to want to keep Gabby home with them, either.

Tears burned behind her eyelids and she fought them back with an effort. Crying wasn't going to change the past. Tears wouldn't bring her mother back or help Richard now. She needed to take action. She had to get to the hospital as soon as possible.

She wiped her damp eyes and turned to look for Shane. He wasn't in the living room or kitchen, so she headed down the hall to Richard's office.

"Oh, no," she whispered when she saw the mess. "Here, too?"

Shane turned and offered a lopsided smile. "Yeah, but we need to dust for prints before we can see if there's anything missing."

She shook her head and folded her arms across her chest. "I won't be any help here," she told him in a plaintive voice. "I've never lived in this house, and haven't been here in years, either."

Shane gestured to the papers lying on top of the desk. "So you didn't know your stepfather was in financial trouble?"

He was? Her stomach churned and Gabby thrust an impatient hand through her hair. "No, how would I know that? I pay his mortgage and that's all. We…haven't spoken to each other in two years. Since the day of my mother's funeral."

Shane's gaze filled with compassion and she turned away, uncomfortable with his scrutiny. "I need a ride back to the hospital. Are you willing to take me—or should I call a cab?"

"I'll take you," he said. "But sometime this afternoon, we'll need you to come down to the station to give a statement. Both on the break-in at your house and for what transpired here."

"Okay, but I don't know much. And I'd like

to stop back by my house to pack an overnight bag, if you don't mind."

"Of course, that's no problem." Shane held out his hand and she surprised herself by accepting it.

His hand was warm and strong, his fingers gently cradling hers. Gabby sucked in a quick breath. She shouldn't be this affected by a simple touch…maybe her long shift was still impacting her ability to think clearly.

Although the usual anxiety she experienced around men wasn't as noticeable with Shane, she was different from the naive resident she was back when she'd gone out with Damon. She was strong and independent. She took pride in what she'd accomplished so far in her career. And she had more milestones to achieve.

Letting down her guard to become close to a man again *wasn't* one of them.

Besides, she told herself that Shane was just being a gentleman, that she shouldn't take his protectiveness as an indication that he thought she was weak. It occurred to her that dealing with violence and crime was Shane's world, far different from working in the hospital where she had everything she needed at her fingertips.

Gabby stole a glance at him, then quickly looked away. She was just another civilian Shane wanted to keep safe, nothing more. Their paths had only crossed in the first place because he needed medical care. And then because she'd needed to be rescued.

Pure circumstance.

She walked with Shane outside, inwardly sighing when she noticed several neighbors standing outside on their porches blatantly watching. Shane informed the other deputy where they were headed.

Nate grimaced. "Griff isn't going to like it that you didn't stick around."

"Tell Griff I'm bringing Gabby in to give her statement, after she checks on her stepfather."

"Okay, but he's still not going to be happy," Nate muttered darkly.

Gabby tugged at her hand, trying to break free, but Shane simply looked at her questioningly. "I think it's better if I take a cab," she said. "I don't want you to get in trouble."

"Don't worry, Griff's bark is worse than his bite," Shane said. "I'm not letting you go back to your place alone."

Truthfully, she wasn't thrilled with the idea of doing that, either. She had her cedar box in Shane's car—did she really need anything else? Wearing something besides scrubs would be nice, but not at the expense of Shane's career.

"Gabby, let's go," Shane urged. "The sooner we pick up your things and check on Richard, the sooner we can get to the station."

"All right," she agreed.

The trip to her house didn't take long and Gabby worked quickly, packing comfortable clothes, toiletries and a blow-dryer into a duffel bag. Suddenly, she hesitated. She normally didn't wear makeup, mostly because she didn't want to draw unwanted male attention to herself.

So why was she suddenly wishing for girlie cosmetics now?

For Shane? Absolutely not.

"I'm ready." She entered the living room, her duffel bag slung over one shoulder.

"Here, let me take that for you," Shane said, reaching for the bag.

Gabby wasn't used to being with someone like Shane, chivalrously opening doors for her, offering to carry her things. Damon had certainly never done any of that. And in the years since, the men she worked with expected her to carry her own weight, no matter what the circumstance. As a result, she'd learned that the only way to be accepted was to be the best.

"Thanks," she said, wondering if she was losing her mind. *Focus.* She needed to focus. And *not* on Shane.

They walked back outside and Gabby checked to make sure she had her spare set of keys, including her car keys, before locking up.

"I'll drop you off at the entrance to the ER and then find a place to park," Shane said as he drove the short distance to the hospital. "Then I'll meet you inside, okay?"

"Sure." She jammed the cedar box into her duffel before climbing out of the car.

"I'll bring that in for you," Shane protested. "Just check on your stepdad, okay?"

"All right." She shut the door and hurried inside, her stomach knotting with anxiety. One glance at the large ER census board told her that Richard was listed as a patient in trauma bay number four, which meant he was still being examined. Had his scans been completed yet? She hurried over to see for herself what was going on.

"Cut back on his IV fluids," Bill Mullen was saying as she entered. "And I want a bed for him on the neuro step-down unit."

Gabby frowned. "Not the ICU?" she asked, coming over to stand beside the tall, lean neurosurgeon.

"You can see the results of the CT scan yourself," Bill said in a reassuring voice. "His subdural bleed is very small…he should recover just fine." The knot in her stomach relaxed a bit. "Has he woken up yet?"

"No, but he's moving all his extremities, so I'm sure he'll come around soon."

"He's been assigned bed five on the neuro step-down unit," one of the nurses informed her. "Do you need anything else before we send him upstairs?"

"Give me a minute to talk to him," Gabby said.

Bill nodded his agreement, so she walked over to Richard's bedside and took his frail hand in hers. "Richard? It's me, Gabby. You're at the hospital and you're going to be just fine. I have the best doctors and nurses taking care of you. Squeeze my hand if you can hear me."

For a moment nothing happened, but then her stepfather's fingers weakly squeezed her hand.

A wave of relief washed over her. Richard wasn't hurt as badly as she'd thought. Bill was an excellent neurosurgeon and she trusted his judgment.

But even though she knew Richard would likely pull through this, she wasn't at all sure that his memory would be intact when he woke up. She knew from other patients she'd cared for that it was rare that they retained any memory of the events preceding a head injury.

Had Richard known his attacker? Did Creighton go over to Richard's house himself or hire someone else to do it? And what was he looking for?

She had no idea. All she could do was to cooperate with the police investigation. Shane was a good cop, and she believed that he'd figure out who was behind all this and why.

"Hey, are you all right?" Shane asked softly, coming up to stand beside her.

She turned toward him and forced a smile.

"Yes, I'm fine. Richard's condition is stable at the moment, and they're getting ready to send him up to the neuro intermediate-care unit. That's a step down from intensive care."

"Good, I'm glad to hear it. I'll need to talk to him once he wakes up."

Gabby swallowed a lump in her throat. "I know."

"Dr. Gabby? We're ready to move him upstairs," the nurse said.

She stepped back, giving the nurses room to maneuver Richard's gurney out from the trauma bay.

"Do you need anything from your bag before we leave?" Shane asked. "I put it in the call room you were in last night."

She wouldn't have minded changing her clothes but shook her head. "No, that's fine. Let's go."

Shane took her arm and once again they walked outside to his police vehicle. Oddly enough, she was getting used to driving around beside him.

Don't go there, she told herself sternly. This entire interlude was just a blip in her routine existence. Soon, everything would be back to normal.

"I'm glad your stepfather is going to be okay," Shane said as he pulled out of the parking structure.

"Me, too. Although, as I mentioned before, I don't know how much help I'll be when it comes to going through his office. You'd be better off waiting for him to wake up so he can tell you what, if anything, is missing."

Shane nodded brusquely. "I don't like the idea of waiting, but it's going to take time for the crime scene techs to get through there anyway, so maybe the delay won't matter."

Gabby hoped they'd find something useful, too. She fell silent as Shane drove to the sheriff's department headquarters, located just a few miles from the hospital.

She followed him inside, glancing around curiously. She'd never been inside a police station or sheriff's department before.

Nate was there, waiting for them. He jerked his thumb behind him. "Griff is waiting for you in his office," he said.

If Shane was worried about getting yelled at, he didn't show it. "Gabby, Nate is going to take your statement, okay? I'll come find you when I'm finished."

She felt nervous but pushed the useless emotion aside since she knew she hadn't done anything wrong. Nate took her into a sterile room that contained metal chairs and a long metal table. He set down a tape recorder and then took a seat across from her.

"I need to record this interview," he said, turning on the machine.

Gabby scowled. "You need my permission," she reminded him, well aware of the Wisconsin state law that protected citizens from being recorded without their consent.

Nate lifted a bow. "Why wouldn't you agree, unless you have something to hide?"

She took another deep breath. "I don't have anything to hide, but you still need to ask for my permission."

Nate stared at her for a long minute. "Okay, do I have your permission to record this interview?"

"Yes." Gabby knew she was being stubborn, but for some reason, Nate's attitude toward her was anything but warm and fuzzy. She didn't understand why he didn't like her, not that it mattered. He was probably just following standard police protocol. And, for all she knew, the only reason Shane treated her better was because of the medical care she'd provided while he was undercover.

Nate's questions started innocuously enough, basic facts about how long she'd lived here in Milwaukee, when she'd graduated from college and then medical school. But then his inquiries became pointed.

"When did you first meet Creighton?"

She stared at him for a long moment. "I've never met Creighton and I don't know who he is."

"You never borrowed any money from him, say, to attend medical school?" the deputy pressed.

That almost made her laugh. "I was given a full scholarship to attend college and took out loans for medical school. I'm still paying off the loans, and if you need proof, I'm happy to provide the paperwork."

"So you did borrow money," Nate said, leaning forward and pinning her with a look. "Maybe you found yourself in over your head and needed a way out? So you took money from Creighton and now he wants it back? Is that it?"

"No, that's *not* it," Gabby said firmly, although she twisted her fingers together at the clear disbelief in the lawman's steely gaze.

She was shocked and horrified to realize that Nate didn't trust in her innocence. He didn't think she was a victim. He actually believed that she knew who Creighton was and what he wanted. And if Nate didn't trust her, Shane probably didn't, either.

Once again, she was on her own.

SIX

Shane approached his boss, trying hard not to let his trepidation show. "Griff."

"Hawk. Sit down." The lieutenant waved a hand at his computer. "I've reviewed your report and I have a couple of follow-up questions."

Shane nodded and took the empty chair. He'd written the report in the wee hours of the morning, could be he forgot a few things. "Okay. Like what?"

"You mentioned you saw Dr. Fielding walking away from the hospital toward the parking structure and you decided to follow her. Why?"

Shane mentally kicked himself for not covering up that detail better, but there was nothing to do now but to tell the truth. "I recognized her because she saved my life six months ago when I was wounded and undercover. I was trying to catch up to her so I could thank her."

Griff scowled. "That's my next question. Do you have a personal relationship with the doc?"

"No!" His instinctive denial came out stronger than he intended. He tried to scale it back. "Trust me, I'm not personally involved with Dr. Fielding. But I do think she's in danger."

"Yeah, I figured that out when she was kidnapped from the hospital parking garage," Griff said in a droll tone.

"And after her house was broken into, and her stepfather was attacked," Shane added. "His house was searched, too, but we don't have any way of knowing if the intruder found what he was looking for."

"So what's your gut telling you?" That was part of the problem. Shane wasn't willing to trust his gut instincts at the risk of being wrong and exposing Gabby to danger. But he'd told Griff he wasn't personally involved with her, so he had to tell his boss something.

"There are two highly likely scenarios," he said slowly. "One is that her stepfather was the real target all along and he's the one involved, either having something Creighton wants or maybe because he's involved in something illegal. The other theory is that the stepfather was just collateral damage and Dr. Fielding is still the intended target. And if that's the case, she remains in danger."

"And you don't think she's involved in something illegal?" Griff prodded. "Or that she knows what this Creighton guy wants?"

"No, sir, I don't." Shane tried to think of a way to convince the lieutenant to believe in Gabby's innocence. "I was there at the scene. She stabbed the gunman and ran into the woods. When I came up behind her, she was terrified. Afterward, she kept trying to tell us that she was kidnapped by mistake."

"Is that so?" Griff leaned his elbows on the desk and steepled his fingers in front of him. "Did you buy her story?"

Shane shook his head. "Obviously, that's not the case since this guy searched her house. But she truly seemed perplexed as to why she was grabbed. I think we have to take a step back, looking at all possibilities." He cleared his throat. "When I questioned her further about her past, she mentioned an old boyfriend that she broke up with and two residents who bitterly resented her intelligence and success. None of the three are named Creighton, but I'd like to do background checks on these guys, at least then we can rule them out as being involved."

Griff stared at him for a long moment, to the point Shane grew restless. It was always hard to tell what his boss was thinking. Shane knew it was a stretch to think that one of these guys from Gabby's past had hired someone named Creighton, who then in turn hired thugs to kidnap her. But he'd feel better if he covered every possibility.

Bottom line: He wasn't going to make *any* assumptions when it came to her safety.

"Okay, fine," Griff said gruffly. "I'll let you do the background checks, but you'd better include the stepfather, too, just in case your first theory is correct. Sounds to me like the old man could be the ultimate target."

Maybe, but he wasn't ready to go there, because he needed to make sure Gabby was safe. And the wave of relief that Griff had given him the go-ahead to continue the investigation shouldn't have been so overwhelming. "Thank you, sir."

"By the way, we got a hit off the fingerprints from one of the three dead gunmen. The one who you identified as the driver is a guy by the name of Curt Wilkens. Did time about five years ago for armed robbery." He shrugged his shoulders and sighed. "We don't have much intel yet about what he was doing in the nine months that he's been out on parole—or how Creighton found him—but so far, he's the only solid lead we have."

Shane nodded slowly. "I'll see if Gab—er—Dr. Fielding recognizes that name."

"Her memory should come in handy, *if* she's telling the truth."

Shane clenched his jaw but didn't argue. "Interesting that we didn't get a hit on the other two. Where do you think Creighton found them?"

"Good question for you to figure out."

"Will do."

Shane started to rise to his feet, but Griff pinned him with a narrow gaze. "Hawk, before you go, write up your statement about the sequence of events that occurred when you arrived at the stepfather's house."

"Of course. I'll do that in my office." Shane headed to his workspace, ignoring the urge to check in to see how Gabby was doing. Nate was likely making her write down her statement, too. He took a seat at his computer and booted up the machine.

The tiny circle on the screen seemed to spin forever before the system flashed on. He typed like a madman, getting all the information down as fast as he could. It wasn't until he sent the report electronically and hit the print button that he realized why he was in such a rush.

He was driven by the need to return to Gabby.

Taking a deep breath and letting it out slowly didn't help make the urge to be near her go away. And even though he knew that he couldn't afford to be personally invested in Gabby, he couldn't deny that he was attracted to her.

An attraction he refused to act on. She was his responsibility, a woman he'd promised to protect. Nothing more.

And maybe if he told himself that over and

over again, he'd find a way to pound that knowledge into his thick skull.

Nate Freemont's intense stare was obviously intended to intimidate her but Gabby kept her emotional turmoil hidden behind a mask of indifference. She'd learned a long time ago to suppress her feelings, ever since the tender age of nine when she'd been thrust into the highly competitive environment at the Einstein School of Brilliance. As the youngest student in residence, she quickly realized that showing any kind of emotion was displaying a sign of weakness. A weakness that other pupils wouldn't hesitate to use to their advantage. She also learned to become impervious to their jeers and insults, remaining strong in order to survive.

Attending medical school and working through her residency as a female surgeon in a male-dominated career hadn't been much different. Even after Damon's assault and the subsequent rumors he'd spread about her, she'd kept her emotions tightly under wraps.

"I'll need you to write your statement," Nate said, pushing a pad of paper and a pen toward her.

She could type faster than she could write but sensed Nate didn't care to make things easy for her. She picked up the pen and began to detail the events that were clearly etched in her memory.

The grim-faced deputy didn't say anything, waiting patiently for her to complete her report. Because her brain was wired to catalog every minute detail, the process took a long time.

The door behind her opened and the back of her neck prickled with awareness as she caught a whiff of Shane's woodsy aftershave. She told herself to ignore him, but it wasn't easy. She paused, momentarily distracted from what she'd been writing.

Seriously, she really needed to get her emotions back under control. Especially since she knew she couldn't afford to trust Shane. Personally or professionally.

She focused on completing the account of what she remembered and shoved the pad of paper toward Nate. "There you go. Let me know if you have any questions."

His eyebrows rose as he scanned the three pages she'd written. "Uh, no questions. I think this covers everything."

"Great, then you don't mind if I head over to the hospital?"

Shane cleared his throat. "Actually, Gabby, would you mind going back to your stepfather's house with me first? The techs have found something interesting and I'd like your input."

She turned to glance at him in surprise. "What did they find?"

"They found some documents in Richard's

study." He avoided her gaze in a way that put her instincts on red alert. "It's hard to explain— I'd rather show you."

Gabby knew that she should return to the hospital to check on her stepfather, but at the same time, she needed to see what had been found in his office. She hadn't known that Richard was in financial trouble, although frankly, she wasn't surprised. Richard was all about looking and acting wealthy even when he wasn't.

"All right," she conceded warily. "I'll go with you to his place."

"Great." Shane turned toward Nate. "You're the computer whiz, will you start on the background checks? And did you hear that we got an ID on one of the dead men?"

Nate grimaced and nodded. "I heard, although we don't know much about what Wilkens was up to."

"So you'll do the background checks?" Shane persisted.

"Sure, why not?"

"Thanks." Shane bent over and scribbled the names she'd given him on the pad of paper. "I'll be in touch."

She followed Shane back outside to his vehicle. It was on the tip of her tongue to ask about his meeting with Griff, but she held back, reminding herself that Shane didn't need her interfering with his job.

Once they were seated and ready to go, Shane glanced at her. "How did things go with Nate?"

"Fine, considering he doesn't trust me."

Shane's brows pulled together in a deep frown. "What do you mean, he doesn't trust you?"

Was Shane being sincere? Or trying to trap her into saying something to implicate herself? "He thinks that I know Creighton and that I took money from him to pay for my outstanding loans that Creighton now wants back."

"Oh, brother," Shane muttered. He sent her a sidelong glance. "Gabby, did you borrow money from Creighton?"

"No. But I do have medical school loans that I'm paying off. The details of which I'm sure Nate will investigate," she said bluntly. Better that she tell Shane everything, before he found out for himself. "He'll find that my entire salary goes toward paying living expenses for myself, my student loans and Richard's mortgage."

"I'm sure everything is in order," Shane said mildly. "Don't be too hard on Nate—all cops tend to be suspicious by nature."

"Including you?"

He nodded. "Yes. But I like to deal in facts and so far none of the facts point to you directly."

His statement caught her off guard. Did this mean that Shane *did* trust her?

Or was that wishful thinking on her part?

Turning away to stare out the window, she

blew out an indignant breath. Why did she care so much about what Shane thought of her?

Ten minutes later, he pulled up in front of Richard's house. The driveway was still blocked with vehicles belonging to the crime scene techs, so she followed Shane as he cut across the front lawn to reach the front door.

After they walked inside the house, she noticed a crime scene tech waiting for them, holding a batch of papers in his gloved hand. "Hey, Hawk," he said by way of greeting.

"Hey, Matt. Thanks for calling. No prints on those?" Shane asked.

Matt shrugged. "Time will tell, although I suspect the ones we found so far belong to the home owner. We have what we need off this, and I thought the information here might be pertinent to your investigation."

Gabby's stomach clenched as she sat down on the sofa beside Shane. She had no reason to be nervous; whatever trouble her stepfather was in didn't have anything to do with her.

"This is odd," Shane murmured. He glanced over at her and then handed her a smudged marriage certificate. "Says here that your mother's last name was Bennett prior to her marriage to your stepfather."

The tension increased, causing her head to throb painfully. She kept her hands in her lap, refusing to take or even look at her mother's marriage certificate. "Yes, that's correct."

"So where does your last name of Fielding come from?" Shane prodded.

The pain in her temples increased to the point she pressed her fingers against her scalp in an effort to ease the ache. "My father's last name was Fielding. My *real* father," she clarified weakly as nausea rose in her throat. "I'm sorry, but I think I'm going to be sick…"

She leaped off the sofa and bolted down the hall to the bathroom, splaying the palm of her hand against her stomach as if she could keep the contents in place by sheer will alone. She hung her head over the sink, closing her eyes against the stabbing pain in her head and breathing deep to combat the queasiness.

It had been years since she'd suffered such terrible migraines. They'd plagued her as a child, but over time, they'd occurred less and less.

But remembering her father, and the way she and her mother had been forced to leave Las Vegas over twenty years ago, brought the crippling headache back with a vengeance.

Despite her eidetic memory, she honestly didn't remember much about that time. Her clearest memory was being instructed by two men in official uniforms to keep the circumstances of their leaving Las Vegas a deep dark secret.

And she hadn't breathed a word to anyone in the ensuing years.

Until now. Because she knew Shane wouldn't rest until she'd told him everything.

Perplexed, Shane stared after Gabby's departing figure, wondering what had made her suddenly feel ill. Was it possible that everything had caught up with her all at once? A delayed reaction from being kidnapped at gunpoint?

He looked back down at the marriage certificate Gabby had brushed against when she'd jumped up from the couch. Gabby had turned pale when he'd mentioned her mother's last name of Bennett. It seemed obvious that if her father's last name was Fielding, that her mother must have been married to someone before Richard Strawn.

To Creighton? Was the guy who'd kidnapped Gabby actually Creighton Bennett?

Shane shot to his feet, unable to believe how wrong he'd been. Considering her photographic memory, Gabby surely knew the name of the man her mother had been married to before Richard.

And he'd been a total idiot to have bought her claim that she didn't know anyone by that name.

He strode purposefully across the room toward the guest bathroom at the end of a short hallway, not far from Richard's office. Remaining calm wasn't easy. "Gabby? Are you all right?"

He heard water running for a long minute before she responded in a muffled voice. "Yes. I'll be right there."

Shane paced the small hallway, glancing at his watch twice before the bathroom door opened, revealing Gabby's pale and drawn face.

"I need to sit down," she said, brushing past him to return to the living room.

His anger faded a bit when he saw how terrible she looked. Maybe there was more to the story. He reined in his temper but sat down on the other end of the sofa, leaving a considerable space between them.

"Tell me what's going on," he said. "Who was your mother married to before Richard?"

Gabby's wide green eyes narrowed with confusion. "What do you mean? She was married to my father and then to Richard. Although I was shocked that she married Richard so soon. Barely six months after she met him."

He hardened his heart against the anguish in her gaze. "Stop it," he said sharply. "Why can't you be honest with me? There's no reason to keep lying. Your mother married Creighton Bennett before she married Richard, isn't that right? Maybe Creighton was a terrible man. Maybe he abused your mother and she ran away. I tried to explain this to you before, Gabby. You need to tell me the truth now, otherwise you're just digging yourself deeper into a web of lies."

Oddly enough, he was glad to see the fire in her eyes replace the wounded confusion. "Don't be ridiculous!" she snapped. "You don't know what you're talking about. I told you I don't know Creighton. And my mother didn't marry anyone else between my father and Richard. There wasn't enough time. She remarried less than a year after my father's death."

Was it possible she was telling the truth? In his entire career, Shane had never felt this torn up by a victim.

Maybe because Gabby was more than just another victim.

"I'm not supposed to tell anyone," she said. "But it's clear you don't trust me, so I hope you keep this information confidential. After my father died, my mother and I were taken away from our house by federal marshals."

Federal marshals? He was stunned speechless for a long moment. "Witness protection?" he gritted out. "Why?"

Gabby winced and pressed her fingers more firmly into her temples. "I don't know, and stop glaring at me like that! I was eight years old at the time. What I do remember is that we were told my father had died and that we needed to disappear. So we were given new names and sent across the country to live in Chicago."

Whatever Shane had expected, it wasn't this. "Witness protection," he repeated. "And you don't know anything more about what your father was involved with?"

She winced and squeezed her eyes shut. "No. I'm sorry, but just thinking about that time brings on a terrible migraine." Several moments passed before she finally said, "And what does it matter anyway? That was twenty-one years ago. Nothing that is happening now has anything to do with something that took place back then."

Shane disagreed, but the pain etched in her features concerned him, so he changed the subject. "How did you and your mother end up in Milwaukee?"

"Richard did sales for a national company and traveled a lot back then. He met my mother in Chicago, apparently she was one of his buyers, but his home base was here. When he proposed to my mother, we relocated to Milwaukee. It all happened so fast…" Her voice trailed off, despair shadowing her eyes.

Shane couldn't hold back any longer. He moved closer to wrap his arm around her shoulders. She held herself stiff at first, but then relaxed, resting her forehead on his chest.

Her citrusy scent filled his senses as he gazed down at her, debating with himself on whether or not to believe her.

And more important, whether he could find

a way to convince Griff and Nate to believe her. He knew from past experience the feds never discussed the people they placed into witness protection. They claimed that maintaining supersecrecy, even from other branches of law enforcement, was the main reason they'd never once lost a witness in the entire history of the program.

Which meant they only had Gabby's word to go by.

SEVEN

The throbbing in Gabby's head was so intense, she felt as if her skull might explode from the pressure. In the subconscious portion of her brain she realized she was physically leaning against Shane for support, soaking up his strength instead of being afraid.

She tensed again when he gently smoothed his hand over her back, and she tried to relax, taking several deep breaths. Listening to the steady beat of his heart helped calm her nerves, but obviously she couldn't stay here like this forever. She needed to move, and when she did, the headache would get worse.

It would take more than willpower to make this headache go away.

"Are you okay?" he asked, his deep, husky voice rumbling close to her ear.

"Yes," she whispered, since any and all movement hurt. "I probably need my medication. Will you please take me back to the hospital?"

There was a long pause before he spoke. "Sure. Just give me a few minutes to see if there's anything else that I need from Richard's office before we go."

She was shocked at the urge to curl her fingers into his shirt as if to make him stay. What was wrong with her? Shane needed to do his job and she needed to put distance between them. She pushed herself upright, trying to summon a smile. "Okay. I'll wait here."

His gaze searched hers for a minute as if to make sure she was really all right, before he rose to his feet. She sank back against the sofa cushions and closed her eyes again. Usually darkness helped her migraines, although it had been years since her last one, so she was definitely out of practice in dealing with them.

Relaxation techniques used to help, so she took more slow deep breaths while imagining she was swinging in a hammock by the beach, listening to the waves rolling in.

The pain eased to a more manageable level by the time Shane returned roughly fifteen minutes later. She opened her eyes, not surprised to see he had several thick file folders in his hands.

"Did you find something else?" she asked.

Shane shrugged. "More evidence that your stepfather was in financial trouble. I see lots of money going out and not much coming in. Did Richard like to gamble?"

For a moment the neon sign of a well-known Vegas casino flashed in her mind, immediately followed by a rolling wave of pain. She quickly shoved the image aside. "Not that I'm aware of, although I can't say I'd be surprised. As I mentioned before, we weren't very close."

"Yeah, I remember. You haven't talked to him since your mother's funeral, right?"

She swallowed hard and nodded. "Yes, that's right. Even before then, we weren't a close-knit happy family. Richard liked things to be done his way, which really bothered me. But my mother certainly didn't seem to mind, which only bugged me more. Thankfully, I ended up working most of the holidays anyway, so I had a good excuse to avoid them."

Shane frowned. "I can't imagine not getting together for family events and holidays."

"I know. Your sister, Leah, always talks about how much fun you had together, and she's even more excited now that she's married Isaac." Gabby pushed herself to her feet, wondering why she was telling him all this. Her feelings regarding family, or lack thereof, wasn't at all pertinent to his investigation. "Can we leave now? I'm more than ready to get out of here."

"Do you need help? My hands are full, but you can take my arm," he offered.

"I'm fine." Gabby was determined to walk outside under her own power. She didn't like the way she was falling apart around Shane. First last night, after the kidnapping, when she'd allowed him to carry her inside the hospital to her call room, and now succumbing to a crippling migraine headache.

She was stronger than this. She didn't lean on others for support, not even after a devastating event. Her mission in life was to take care of others, to heal the injured. She was fully capable of looking after herself.

At least she had been, until two men with guns had kidnapped her outside the hospital parking lot. Hours later and the entire incident still seemed surreal.

"Do you want me to drive around to the front of the hospital where the pharmacy is located?" Shane asked.

"No, I have some medication left over in my bag. Although they're a little old, so they might not work as well. But they'll do until I can call my doctor to request a refill on my prescription."

"All right, then we'll head to your call room, since that's where we left your stuff."

"Okay." The thought of going back to the hospital was reassuring. Being questioned by the police, baring her secrets to Shane, wasn't at all part of her comfort zone. But working on trauma patients, being in the OR, reading up on the latest trends in trauma care—that was normal.

She needed to remember that this nightmare

would be over once Shane and his fellow SWAT-team members found Creighton. And it would be in her best interest to help them in any way possible.

The sooner she was able to combat this headache and return to her usual routine, the better.

Shane glanced at Gabby as he pulled into the parking structure. "Are you okay to walk?"

"Of course. I'm fine." Her voice was firm, but her pale face and trembling fingers told a different story.

He could appreciate her stamina and her determination to stand on her own two feet, but it occurred to him that Gabby needed a lot more emotional support than she realized.

Spiritual support, too.

He was relatively new when it came to going to church, but now that he prayed on a regular basis, he couldn't imagine how he'd survived without God's strength and support. But he wasn't an expert on faith and had no idea how to even broach the possibility with Gabby.

Still, having her entire life revolve around work wasn't healthy, so he knew he had to try. Not that he was minimizing her career, far from it. Her chosen profession was admirable. But at what cost?

He couldn't help wondering if her headache was a culmination of pressure and stress. Not that he should care so much either way. His heart wanted to protect her, even though his head told him that was a bad idea.

He escorted Gabby to her call room and propped his shoulder against the door frame as she carefully removed the cedar box of personal items, then rummaged through her duffel for the medication.

"Do you need some time to rest?" he asked gently, after she swallowed the pill.

She grimaced. "I'd like to, but I need to check on Richard. See if there's been any change."

Shane straightened from the door frame. "I'll go with you. If he happens to be awake, I have several questions for him."

Gabby's brow puckered in a frown. "Listen, Shane, in my experience most people with head injuries don't remember much prior to being hurt. Richard may not be able to give you the information you need."

"I understand, but I still need to talk to him. But I won't do anything that interferes with his ability to get better, okay? If he becomes upset, I'll stop."

"Okay." Gabby slowly rose to her feet. "Let's go."

Shane wished he could force her to rest, but all he could do was to follow as she led the way through a maze of corridors to the other side of the hospital. She took the elevators to the fifth floor and then walked down a corridor to a room that had her stepfather's name outside the door.

She paused, as if to gather her strength, before pushing the door open. "Richard?" she called in a soft voice. "It's me, Gabriella."

There was no response from the patient stretched out on the bed. Richard Strawn looked older, more fragile against the white sheets, wearing a hospital gown and a bandage over the wound on his temple.

Shane hung back as Gabby stepped up to the bed. She reached down and took Richard's hand in hers. "The doctors and nurses are taking good care of you," she murmured. "I made sure to ask for the best."

Richard still didn't respond, and Shane heard Gabby sigh. She glanced at him over her shoulder. "He won't be answering questions anytime soon."

Yeah, he got that. He swallowed his frustration at the fact that their best lead was lying unconscious and might never remember anything that could help them find Creighton. "Do you think his head injury is worse?"

"I don't know," she whispered helplessly, turning back to stare down at her stepfather.

Shane stepped up beside her and gently squeezed her shoulder. "We should pray for him," he suggested in a low voice.

"Pray?" Her startled gaze caught his. "I don't

know much about that. And I don't know that Richard believes in God, either."

He shifted, feeling a little embarrassed, but at the same time, he didn't want to back down. "Well, I do believe and I think it's important for us to pray for him."

She hesitated but then nodded. "All right." She bowed her head and clasped her hands in front of her.

Relieved that she hadn't refused outright, Shane closed his eyes for a moment, searching his heart for the proper words. "Dear Lord, we ask that You please heal Richard's injury with Your grace and goodness. Also we ask that You continue to provide knowledge and strength to the doctors and nurses caring for him. And please help guide us on Your chosen path. Amen."

"Amen," Gabby echoed.

Shane was touched that she'd responded verbally to his prayer and hoped that she'd found a little peace, especially after everything she'd been through.

"Do you want to talk to his doctor again?" he asked when she remained quiet beside him.

"Not right now." She hesitated then asked, "Do you really think God cares about whether or not Richard recovers from his injury?"

Shane nodded. "Yes, I do. God cares about all of His children, even those who may not have found their way to Him yet." *Like you*, he almost added, catching himself in the nick of time.

Gabby glanced up at him and he was relieved to see that the haze of pain had faded a bit from her eyes. Maybe her medication had kicked in, after all. "I don't think Richard has been going to church on a regular basis."

He shrugged. "But there's always a first time," he pointed out. "If Richard recovers, he may decide that faith is important, especially after this close brush with death."

"Maybe," Gabby said, although her gaze was full of doubt. "I haven't really thought about God and faith much over the years. When my mother was placed in hospice care after her treatment for colon cancer failed, her pastor came to visit. Richard scowled at the poor guy the entire time, so the pastor didn't stay long."

Shane's heart went out to her. Losing her mother to cancer couldn't have been easy for her. "I'm sorry that you had a bad experience, but I believe that your mother may have gotten the prayers and support she needed to be at peace with her death."

"She did seem to be at peace with her decision. She refused more chemo once the cancer had spread to her liver and kidneys," she admitted. "Richard blamed me for the way she gave up because I was honest with her regarding her chances of surviving."

Shane tried to squelch a flash of anger on Gabby's behalf. "He was just lashing out at you because of his grief, nothing more."

Gabby grimaced but continued to stare down at her stepfather. "In the past few years, I've watched many family members pray for their loved ones. I always imagined they were part of a close-knit family who truly cared about each other. I have to confess, I never expected to be here like this for Richard."

"Faith can be comforting for both the patient and their family members." Shane fought the urge to put his arm around Gabby's shoulders to offer comfort. He curled his fingers over the side rail, instead. "Gabby, I know that you and your stepfather haven't been close, but it's important to forgive those who have hurt us. We should try to be like God and Jesus, who forgave those who had forsaken and betrayed him. He would like us to try to do the same."

Gabby was silent for a long moment. "You don't know what you're asking," she said finally.

"I know it's not easy—in fact, I'm still struggling with the concept of forgiveness too," he told her. "My fiancée left me six months before our wedding for another man."

Gabby's eyes widened in shock. "That's terrible."

"Yeah, it wasn't fun, and I lost a couple grand

as a side bonus. For years I resented her, but since I've started attending church, I've been working on forgiveness."

"I give you a lot of credit for being able to do that," Gabby said. She stepped back from the bedside and he wasn't surprised when she changed the subject. "My headache is still lingering, so I think I'll return to my call room for a while."

"I'll walk you back," Shane offered, disappointed at the way she was pulling away from him.

"Suit yourself," she said, turning and heading toward the door.

He followed her as she made her way to the call room, once again taking back hallways and stairwells that were used only by hospital staff.

Shane knew he should be happy that she'd agreed to pray with him at all, but he couldn't help wishing for more. Clearly, whatever had caused the rift between Gabby and her stepfather was something so bad that she couldn't readily find forgiveness.

Getting romantically involved with Gabby wasn't an option, but he couldn't ignore the fact that she needed help finding a way to God and faith.

And if he could manage a way to accomplish that, while keeping her safe at the same time, he would force himself to be satisfied with that.

* * *

Gabby was far too conscious of Shane's presence beside her as she headed for the call room. Her headache still plagued her, but not nearly as badly as it had earlier.

Shane's words about forgiveness echoed over and over in her mind. Trying to find a way to forgive Richard was one thing.

Forgiving Damon for nearly raping her was something completely different.

"Do you want something to eat?" Shane asked as they passed the cafeteria.

Her stomach lurched and twisted. "No, thanks. But you can grab something if you like. There's no reason to follow me back to my call room."

Shane shrugged. "I'll grab something later."

She suppressed a sigh and rubbed her temple. When one of her colleagues, Dr. Noah Graham, walked out of the cafeteria, she was surprised when he called out to her. "Gabby? Do you have a minute?"

"Sure." She stopped and turned toward him. "What's up?"

Noah glanced pointedly at Shane. "Do you mind? This is a private conversation about a patient."

Shane crossed his arms over his chest, impressive in his uniform. "I do mind...I'm not leaving. Don't use patient names and I won't pay attention to the details."

Gabby glanced between the two men with a scowl. "Stop it, both of you. What do you need, Noah?"

"Remember our patient with the low abdominal wound from last night?" he asked, stepping to the side and turning so that his back was facing Shane.

"Yes, I remember. Why? What happened?"

"He took a turn for the worse, and I need to take him back to the OR. I thought you might want to assist."

Truthfully, all she wanted was to rest so that the last remnants of her headache faded away, but she forced herself to nod. "Sure, no problem. What time?"

"I'm heading up to the OR now," Noah said.

She glanced over at Shane, who did not look at all happy. "I have to go. I'll see you later."

"How long will this take?" he asked.

"An hour or two at the most. But you don't need to stick around."

"I'll wait for you," he said firmly.

She didn't argue, especially since she didn't want Noah to know anything about the real reason Shane was there. "Okay, I'll come down here to find you."

Noah headed toward the elevators and she followed, glancing back to where Shane stood, watching them.

"New boyfriend?" Noah asked as he pressed the elevator button.

It was on the tip of her tongue to deny it, but for some odd reason she hesitated. Maybe having people believe they were dating was a better way to salvage her reputation than having everyone know that she'd been kidnapped and might still be in danger.

"We're friends," she said, finally breaking the long silence.

"Sure, whatever you say," Noah retorted with a smirk. "Friends."

She refused to react, keeping her expression impassive as they walked into the operating room and began to scrub for their case. Once in the OR suite, years of training took over, crowding everything out of her mind, including her migraine.

The patient's abdominal wound didn't look good, and as they worked she realized that they must have missed a metal fragment that was lodged in the patient's colon. Had it been her fault? She hadn't been the primary surgeon, but she had assisted long enough to stop the bleeding.

She swallowed the lump of guilt and concentrated on making sure the wound was irrigated with antibiotic solution before closing the incision for a second time. An hour later, she stepped back from the OR table. "That should do it," she said.

"Thanks," Noah replied, barely glancing at her. Did he blame her in some way? She was tired of fighting against the bias many of her male colleagues had against female surgeons.

Gabby left the OR and stripped out of her sterile garb. She scrubbed again at the sink before going into the women's locker room for clean scrubs. Then she headed back down to the cafeteria to meet Shane.

He was sitting at a table right near the cafeteria entrance, and their gazes locked as she approached. The tingle of awareness that shot down her spine caught her by surprise. Shane exuded an inner strength and confidence that she'd never experienced with her male colleagues.

"Everything all right?" Shane asked, rising to his feet to meet her.

She nodded, disconcerted by his nearness. His powerful frame was overwhelming yet comforting at the same time. "Yeah, fine." The scent of food made her realize that her headache was nearly gone and that she was hungry, after all.

But before she could head in to pick something up to eat, the loudspeaker overhead came on. "Code blue, fifth floor, room twenty-one."

Gabby gasped and clutched Shane's arm. "That's Richard's room."

"Let's go," he said.

She was already running toward the stairwell, refusing to wait for the elevator.

What could possibly have happened to her stepfather? He'd been stable a mere hour ago. Maybe Shane was right, maybe this was the time to try to forgive Richard.

Or was it already too late?

EIGHT

Shane kept pace with Gabby as she took the five flights of stairs up to her stepfather's room with the gracefulness and energy of a gazelle. She was absolutely incredible, especially after everything she'd been through. No one would ever know that she'd been kidnapped, questioned by the police, spent over an hour in the OR performing surgery, all while dealing with a terrible headache.

Completely amazing.

He tried to reel in his emotions, knowing that this attraction simmering in his bloodstream for Gabby was dangerous. On more than one level. Not just for himself, personally. But professionally. He couldn't afford to lose his ability to be impartial, not while working this case.

Not until they knew the truth about Creighton. And any potential ties to Gabby's past. While Gabby had been in the OR, he'd reported in to Griff and Nate about how she'd stated that she and her mother were placed in witness protection.

Of course, Griff and Nate were skeptical. And he couldn't blame them. Still, at this point, nothing else explained the different name on Gabby's mother's marriage certificate.

They'd know for sure as soon as Nate finished his background checks.

When they reached the fifth floor, there was a crowd of people standing outside Richard's room. Gabby's face went pale as they approached. She stopped just outside the door to her stepfather's room, watching as the medical team worked on her stepfather, with her hand covering her mouth. Ten minutes later, she swayed and he quickly slipped his arm around her waist to hold her upright.

"Let's find a place to sit down," he urged.

"No, I'm fine," Gabby said, stiffening her spine. She allowed him to stand beside her for another few moments before she stepped forward. "Bill?" she called over the mob of people. "What's going on? What happened?"

Shane recognized the tall, lean neurosurgeon who had met Gabby in the ER when her stepfather was first being examined. The neurosurgeon edged through the crowd toward her. "He went into V-tach, and then V-fib. We've shocked him, but without success. Things don't look good. I'm sorry, Gabby."

"I don't understand," she murmured, her arms crossed protectively across her chest. "His vitals were stable. His head injury wasn't that serious. What could have happened?"

"I'm not sure what to tell you," Bill admitted, appearing just as frustrated as Gabby was. "We have his code labs back and his potassium levels are pretty high, but that could be because of his heart attack. We've given him meds to bring his potassium levels down, but that hasn't helped. At this point, the only other explanation so far is that he threw some sort of blood clot. And since he has a head injury, we can't afford to give him any blood thinners."

Gabby thrust her fingers through her hair and Shane stepped closer to her side, just in case.

"Still in asystole," someone said loudly from inside the room. "Continue CPR."

The neurosurgeon turned to go back inside the patient's room. For several long moments the team continued to work on Richard in spite of the fact that his heart rhythm was nothing more than a straight line.

Finally the neurosurgeon spoke up again. "He's been down for fifteen minutes already with no pulse. I'm calling the code. It's over. Thanks, everyone."

Gabby made a soft sound in the back of her throat, and this time Shane wasn't taking no for an answer. He put his arm around her waist and physically turned her around so he could guide her back toward the patient lounge located at the end of the hallway.

She collapsed onto the cushioned sofa and he sat beside her, staying close. "I'm so sorry, Gabby," he murmured.

"I just can't believe he's gone," she whispered.

"I know," he said, feeling helpless.

"It's my fault he's dead," she said in a choked tone and then surprised him by turning and burying her face in the curve of his shoulder. His heart twisted when he felt the dampness of her tears.

"Don't cry," he said, holding her close. "His death isn't your fault, Gabby. Creighton did this, not you."

There was a long pause and she sniffed loudly as if trying to stop the flow of tears. "Richard resented me, right from the very beginning."

"You were young, Gabby, maybe you misunderstood."

"No, I knew. He wanted my mother all to himself. He arranged for me to be sent away to live at a boarding school when I was nine years old," she said. "I cried, begging him and my mother to let me stay home, but he insisted. And my mother went along with it."

Nine? A surge of anger on her behalf made him see red. Who sent a nine-year-old to boarding school? Especially barely a year after losing her father? "That sounds rough."

She sighed against him. "Yeah. And when I came home for the holidays, Richard made it clear that he and my mother were too busy to spend time with me. They were always heading off to parties and events, leaving me home with a babysitter."

Okay, now he was really starting to dislike the guy. No wonder she hadn't jumped to forgive him. "I'm sorry, Gabby."

"Eventually, I stopped coming home." She sniffed again and reached up to wipe her eyes.

"Staying at school with your friends must have been a little better than going home," he said.

She shook her head against him. "No friends. All the kids at the Einstein School of Brilliance were in competition with each other for the best grades and the best scholarships."

No friends? No family? He couldn't imagine such a thing. How on earth had she survived? He reached down and put his finger beneath her chin, tipping her face up so he could look into her eyes.

"Gabby, you are the most amazing and incredible woman I've ever known," he said huskily.

The corners of her lips turned up in a semblance of a smile. "I'm not, but thanks for saying so."

Since words didn't seem to be getting through

to her, he slowly bent his head, giving her plenty of time to back away, before he tenderly kissed her.

Gabby was caught off guard by Shane's kiss and for a fleeting moment, she enjoyed the sensation of his mouth on hers before old memories flooded her brain, causing her to stiffen and pull away.

Shane's eyes were full of apology. "I'm sorry, I shouldn't have done that."

"No, really, it's just…" Her voice trailed off, as she couldn't bear to tell him the truth. "You took me by surprise. I'm not used to being with a man like this," she finished lamely.

Shane reached up to tuck a stray curl behind her ear. "I only wanted to offer comfort, Gabby, nothing more. I shouldn't have overstepped my boundaries."

"You *have* given me comfort," she admitted shyly. Being with Shane like this didn't scare or frighten her. It was just the memory of Damon's actions that had flashed in her mind, causing her instinctive reaction. A response Shane didn't deserve. "More than anyone else ever has."

"Oh, Gabby," Shane murmured, drawing her close again and tucking her head under his chin. "You tear me up when you say things like that. I don't know how you managed to get through your lonely childhood to become the woman you are today."

She closed her eyes and breathed in his familiar woodsy scent. "I had a teacher, Mary Jane Pollard, who took me under her wing. She was an amazing teacher and mentor. I told her that I wanted to be a trauma doctor when I grew up and she never once tried to talk me out of it. She was a huge support and inspiration for me, even after I left Einstein's to attend medical school."

"I'm glad you had someone like Mary Jane in your life," Shane said softly. "Is she still around? Maybe we should go visit her."

"She's in a nursing home now," Gabby said with a sigh. "She suffered a stroke several years ago. The last time I saw her, she didn't seem to remember me. She was a huge part of my life, but I was just one of many students she taught."

"I bet you were special to her, too," Shane said. "It sounds as if you two bonded for a while there."

Gabby smiled against Shane's broad shoulder, touched by his determination to make her feel better. She wished she could stay in his arms like this forever.

"Gabby?"

Reluctantly she pulled away from Shane to glance up at Bill Mullen. "Yes?"

Bill cleared his throat awkwardly. "I'd like to

do an autopsy, with your permission, of course. I think we need to understand what happened."

She nodded. "I wholeheartedly agree. Maybe we'll find it was a blood clot, or maybe it was something else. I would like to know one way or the other. And I'd appreciate a call when you get the preliminary results back."

The neurosurgeon nodded. "Will do. Unfortunately, we'll need to know the funeral details as well."

Gabby gave him the name of the same funeral home that they'd used when her mother died.

"All right, let me know if you need anything more," Bill said before he turned and walked away.

Shane's phone rang and he answered it, staying right beside her rather than going someplace more private. She tried not to eavesdrop, but it wasn't easy.

"Extended leave of absence, huh?" Shane said, glancing at Gabby. "That is interesting. Can you get me the make and model of the car he drives and the license plate number? Great. Thanks, Nate."

"Who's on an extended leave?" she asked, hoping desperately that he wasn't talking about Damon Keller. She thought she'd put her past behind her.

But her reaction to Shane's kiss had proven otherwise.

"Eric Ambrose," Shane said in a grim tone. "Nate found out that he was working on the East Coast, in Baltimore. And it sounds like he might have gotten himself in trouble, too."

"What kind of trouble?"

"Nate found that Ambrose has a pending medical-malpractice lawsuit against him." Shane's keen blue gaze bore into hers. "Do you know anything about that?"

She shook her head. "No. How could I? You said yourself that he's been out on the East Coast. And you have to understand that filing a lawsuit doesn't take much. People do that all the time. Almost a third never get past the initial filing, mostly because the burden of proof is on the plaintiff."

Shane looked surprised. "You sound like you've had experience with this type of thing."

"Not really, at least not on a personal level. But we had an ethical/legal class in med school that I found very interesting."

"Hmm. So basically, you're telling me this lawsuit doesn't mean much," Shane said with obvious disappointment.

"It's hard to say for sure without knowing the details about the case." Gabby was tempted to stop there but knew he deserved to know her suspicions. "When we were residents, Eric was all about being the best. He wanted the position of senior resident for the trauma program very badly. There was a salary advantage as well as the prestige of the role. He and I were the main two in the running, so he did whatever he could to sabotage me."

Shane scowled. "Sabotage you, how?"

"He and Joe Chasco would give me wrong information during handoffs, trying to make me look bad in front of the attending physician." Gabby still couldn't believe Eric and Joe had risked harming patients just to make themselves look better. "Luckily, I was super conscientious and always looked at my patients' charts for myself. So I was able to avoid their pitiful attempts to humiliate me."

"That's crazy," Shane muttered darkly. "Why would they put patients at risk?"

Gabby shrugged. "Most physicians truly care about their patients. But there is a small minority who go into this career because they care about the money, prestige and power. Eric Ambrose is a prime example of the latter. He was awarded a full scholarship to college, the same way I was. But he wasn't satisfied unless he was the first in his class. And if working hard didn't get him what he wanted, he wasn't above cheating. He couldn't stand the thought of being beaten out for the senior resident position, especially by a woman."

"He sounds like a jerk," Shane said. "Do you

think it's possible that he still resents you, all these years later?"

"Considering I was awarded the position of senior resident four years ago, it's a stretch," Gabby admitted. "However, the fact that he has a pending lawsuit is an interesting twist. And not just the litigation itself, but the fact that the hospital put him on a leave of absence. That's not normal protocol unless they're thinking of taking some sort of employment action against him."

"I see," Shane murmured. "In other words, the lawsuit might have merit."

"Yeah. And if so, it's possible that a hospital defense attorney would dig into Eric's background, looking for ways to discredit him."

"No offense, Gabby, but I can't imagine any attorney risking kidnapping a witness at gunpoint."

"No, not an attorney," she agreed. "But we're talking about a guy who would do anything to keep his reputation intact. I wonder if Eric has been in touch with Joe Chasco."

"Nate found Joe in Chicago and verified that he was working the night you were kidnapped."

"So then it's just Eric we need to worry about. I still think it's possible he believes I'd testify against him in some way."

Narrowing his eyes, Shane tapped a finger against his chin. "You think Eric hired Creighton? Who in turn hired three guys and then killed them all when they failed to turn you over?"

The doubt in Shane's tone made her feel foolish. Logically, she knew this theory wasn't likely. But then again, in her mind, the entire kidnapping was a crazy idea, too. "Maybe."

"I disagree. It doesn't make sense that Eric would go after your stepfather," he pointed out.

"No, it doesn't. Although he could have been looking for my notes."

Shane's head shot up and his gaze pinned hers in an intense glare. "Notes? What notes?"

She tried not to squirm in her seat. "Notes on what he and Joe Chasco did in an attempt to discredit me," she admitted.

"Wait a minute, are you saying Joe and Eric knew you documented what happened?" Shane asked.

"Yes. In fact, I used the notes to threaten them." When Shane's eyebrows levered upward, she sighed. "Look, I needed them to stop, right? I told them I had proof that they lied to me to make me look bad and that I had notes describing every incident that occurred. I told them I kept my notes locked up in a secure spot and that if they didn't knock off their ridiculous antics I'd get them kicked out of the program." She lifted her hands palm upward. "It worked, they left me alone from that point on."

Shane was silent for a long moment. "Okay,

that information does change things a bit. Let's just say that Eric hired Creighton to find this so-called evidence. Evidence that he doesn't want uncovered to be used against him in a lawsuit. He kidnaps you and when that doesn't work, he searches your house and your stepfather's, too. But he's also basically killed four people. Which makes him a sociopath."

Gabby swallowed hard. "Sociopath is a good way to describe him. But keep in mind, that's just my opinion. And since I was his main target, my word isn't exactly unbiased."

"Your opinion is good enough for me," Shane said, jaw muscles flexing. "Nate's working on getting his vehicle information. Once we have that, we'll put out an APB to bring him in as a person of interest."

She nodded. "Okay."

"Anything else I need to know?" Shane asked. "Is there other pertinent information you're not telling me?"

Gabby inwardly winced and dropped her gaze. She didn't really want to tell Shane about Damon's attempted assault. But she didn't want to lie to him, either.

Her pager went off, and she pounced on it like a lifeline. "Excuse me, I need to take this."

She rose to her feet and hurried over to the house phone hanging on the lounge wall to return the call.

NINE

Shane watched Gabby as she spoke on the phone, mentally kicking himself for crossing the line and kissing her. For a moment her lips had clung to his, before she came to her senses and abruptly pulled away. Obviously he'd gone too far, despite her claim to the contrary.

He rubbed the back of his neck, trying to focus on the issue of keeping Gabby safe rather than ruminating on his blunder. After everything Gabby had told him about Eric Ambrose, he was forced to admit that the physician could be the guy they were after.

Especially if he really was a sociopath.

Still, Shane couldn't get the image of those three dead men in the clearing out of his mind. The way they had been shot execution-style reminded him of an organized-crime hit. But what if that's what Ambrose wanted them to think? What if that was his way of throwing suspicion off himself?

He couldn't believe Gabby had kept notes related to the things the two residents had done to discredit her. He frowned, wondering just where those notes were. Must not have been at her house, since she hadn't said anything about them.

His phone rang and when he saw Nate's name, he quickly answered. "Hey, buddy, what's up?"

"I can't get anyone to confirm Gabby and her mother were in witness protection. Not that I really expected to. Those marshals are beyond secretive."

"I know," Shane concurred. "But still, the fact that Gabby's mother had a different last name verifies Gabby's claim. Anything else crop up?"

"I was able to pull some financial information on Richard Strawn. It's pretty clear the guy had a big-time gambling problem. Lots of cash going out at very high levels. Some smaller amounts spent at casinos, too."

"Really?" Shane straightened in his seat, wondering if his first theory had been right all along. "Any idea who he was in debt to?"

"Not yet, but from what I can see he's in for at least fifty grand."

Fifty grand? Far from chump change. Enough to kill for? Maybe.

"Interesting," Shane murmured. "So maybe Creighton is a loan shark and was ticked that Richard didn't pay up?"

"Could be," Nate agreed. "I haven't found any indication that he owes a casino money—those debts seem to be paid—so it seems logical that he used a loan shark for some private poker games or something along those lines. We can ask him about it once he recovers from his head injury."

Shane winced. "Unfortunately not. Richard just passed away."

"He's…dead?" Nate asked in surprise. "What happened? I thought he wasn't hurt that bad."

"Yeah, that's what we thought, too." Sighing, he pinched the bridge of his nose. "The doctor isn't sure what happened. The current theory is that he threw a blood clot. Gabby agreed to an autopsy, but so far there's no indication of foul play."

"Yet," Nate muttered.

"Yeah, yet. Although it seems odd that Creighton would try to finish him off, since dead men can't pay their debts. And there's no sign he was worked over."

"No, but it could be that killing Strawn was Creighton's way of sending a message," Nate said slowly.

A message? To Gabby? A chill snaked down his spine. "Do you think Creighton grabbed Gabby to force her to pay her stepfather's debts? After all, she was paying his mortgage."

"I hadn't considered that possibility," Nate answered. "But it makes sense."

Shane watched as Gabby hung up the phone and wearily ran her fingers through her pretty red curls. How frustrating to have so many suspects and not enough information on any of them. "Any hits on Ambrose's car?" he asked as she crossed back over to where he stood.

"No, it's going to take time. And we don't even know for sure he's in the state of Wisconsin. He could be anywhere."

Yeah. Like Chicago, where Ambrose's sidekick was currently living. Hadn't Gabby said the two residents worked together to set her up? "Check in with the Illinois state troopers," he directed. "I think it's a strong possibility Ambrose might be hanging out in the Chicago area."

"Near his old buddy Joe Chasco? Yeah, you have a point. Sounds good."

"Thanks Nate," Shane said before disconnecting from the call and turning toward Gabby. "Everything all right?" he asked.

She nodded, looking dead on her feet. "Yes, for the most part. Our surgical patient is having some complications, but a change in antibiotic coverage should help." She paused and then asked, "No news on Eric Ambrose?"

"No, but we'll find him," he said, infusing confidence in his tone. He didn't like the shadow of fear that lingered in her eyes and had to resist the urge to give her a hug. "You look like you could use something to eat. Should we go back down to the cafeteria?"

"I'm not hungry and it's getting late. I'd rather get some sleep."

"Okay, that works," Shane agreed. "We can head over to your call room."

Gabby walked toward the stairwell, and Shane followed, having gone this route long enough with her now that he was familiar with the path she liked to take to get from one side of the hospital to the other.

She glanced at him over her shoulder. "Aren't you heading home soon?" she asked. "You've been here over twenty-four hours."

"So have you." He couldn't deny wishing for a soft bed and a shower, but not at the expense of Gabby's safety. "And no, I'm not heading home."

"Shane." The husky note in Gabby's voice as she said his name made him catch his breath, wishing he had the right to hold her close. She stopped on the landing and turned to face him. "You can't keep sleeping on the floor outside my call room. For one thing, it can't be at all comfortable. And for another, I'm safe here inside the hospital. Safer than I'd be anywhere else."

Shane wasn't sure he agreed; he believed an anonymous hotel room might be better. But maybe she didn't feel safe in a hotel room, even if he was staying right next door. And was that different than him staying in a call room next to her? Maybe not.

There was something to be said for being surrounded by people. And security guards, some of whom carried Tasers.

"I'm staying," he repeated firmly. "If there's a spare call room right next to yours, I'd consider that, but if not, the floor will do. I've slept in worse places."

"I'm sure there's an empty call room." Gabby took the stairs the rest of the way down, and as they walked past the cafeteria, she slowed and then turned in to the doorway. "I guess I will pick up something to eat."

Shane strode alongside her, glad she was taking care of herself. At least she seemed to have recovered from the shock of her stepfather's unexpected demise. Maybe being a physician helped her keep things in perspective. She made herself a large salad from the salad bar before walking over to the cashier. When he pulled out his wallet to pay for her meal, Gabby looked as if she might argue, but then allowed him to pay without a protest.

He knew he was going a bit overboard with Gabby. As much as he told himself that he just wanted to protect her, and to keep her safe, he was forced to admit his feelings were much more complicated than that.

He admired her. And was beginning to care about her. Far too much.

Hadn't he learned his lesson with Linda? He'd been totally devastated when he'd found out she was cheating on him. With a detective from their same district, no less.

He'd loved Linda more than she'd loved him. She'd only felt gratitude towards him, nothing more. No way was he going to make the same mistake again.

So despite how much he liked and respected her, Gabby was off-limits. For her sake, as much as his own.

Gabby walked to the suite of on-call rooms, wishing there was a way to convince Shane that he didn't need to stay the night playing bodyguard.

But she knew she'd have more luck talking to a rock. She suspected *stubborn* was Shane Hawkins's middle name.

She paused outside the call room where she'd left her duffel bag earlier that afternoon. The pain in her head was better, although there was still a lingering ache. Nothing she couldn't handle. Still, it seemed as if days had passed since she'd been back here to get her meds, rather than mere hours.

"Is one of the rooms on either side of you open?" Shane asked from behind her.

"I'll call Security to find out." She punched the code into the keypad on the door handle.

"I really need to be right next door," Shane insisted. "If that's not possible, the floor will work fine."

She ground her teeth together in frustration as she pushed the door open. "The floor is *not* fine. Just give me a minute, okay?" Leaving the door ajar, she crossed over to the small bedside table. She turned on the lamp and then picked up the phone.

Security answered and informed her that call rooms ten and eleven were open. The rooms on either side of hers were not. "Please take me out of room five and assign me to rooms ten and eleven, thanks."

She expected the security guard to give her a hard time over needing two rooms, but he didn't object. Had Shane already put the security team on notice about the potential danger? The thought didn't sit well with her, but there wasn't much she could do about it, either.

After hanging up the phone, she picked up her duffel bag and walked back out into the corridor where Shane waited. "We have rooms located at the end of this hall."

"Okay," Shane agreed.

"The doors all have keypad combination locks, and the codes are the full room number located up on the door frame punched in backward."

Gabby demonstrated outside room ten, which was listed on the upper-right door frame as 1010. She put the numbers in backward and the door clicked open. "Do you want this room or the one closest to the stairwell?"

"I'll take the one near the stairwell," Shane said, frowning at the push-button locks. "I'm not sure I like the fact that anyone here could easily find out the code to your room."

Gabby suppressed a sigh. "Only people who work here, the ER staff and the doctors who use the call rooms. These rooms are exclusively reserved for attending physicians—the residents are located closer to the ICU. And we can request the codes to be changed if needed."

"You don't know how to do that yourself?"

"No, why would I? I'd have to call one of the maintenance guys to do that." When she sensed he was about to ask her to go ahead and do just that, her temper flared. "Come on, Shane, this isn't a high-risk area. The only way to get back here is through a back stairwell or through the ER itself. Neither place is easily accessible to the public. Can you honestly say that this is less safe than some random hotel?"

"I guess not," he agreed with apparent reluctance. "But I'm not going to apologize for worrying about your safety. Less than twenty-four hours ago, you were kidnapped at gunpoint from right outside this hospital. I'm here to make sure that doesn't happen again."

The somber note in Shane's tone caused her brief flash of anger to fizzle. "I know," she admitted softly. "Trust me, I'd prefer to be safe, too. And I want you to know how much I appreciate everything you've done for me." She gestured to the room he intended to stay in. "This is going above and beyond the call of duty."

His crooked smile made her tummy do another backflip. "No, it's not. I owe you for saving my life, remember? I doubt I'd be alive if it wasn't for you."

She blushed and shrugged. "You never mentioned who shot you and why."

Shane's expression clouded over. "I was working undercover on an illegal arms case. Unfortunately I eventually found out my boss was dirty. I'm lucky I was only shot and not killed outright."

His boss? "Lieutenant Vaughn?"

"No, my former boss, Lieutenant Nash, from the Milwaukee Police Department. I just recently joined the sheriff's department because I didn't trust anyone at my old district."

"That must have been terrible," she said with a frown.

"Not really. After all, going through all of that is how I met you."

She felt her cheeks growing warm again, but

resisted the urge to cover them with her hands. She couldn't help but be impressed by how Shane was able to put a positive spin on everything he'd endured. And oddly enough, knowing he'd had to overcome adversity, just like she had, gave them something in common.

"Try to get some sleep, Gabby," Shane said, interrupting her thoughts. "We'll talk more in the morning."

She nodded and turned away, feeling the intensity of Shane's gaze on her back as she went into her newly assigned call room and quietly shut the door.

For a moment she stood there, aching for something she didn't dare name. Why was she so attracted to him? Shane wasn't like any of the men she worked with. And not just because he believed in God and prayer, although that was certainly a rarity in her experience.

He was different in the way he treated her, as if she was special. And not supersmart special, either. She wished so much that she hadn't pulled away from his kiss.

Because she wanted a chance to repeat that kiss. And soon.

Stop it, she told herself sternly. Didn't she have bigger issues to worry about right now than thinking about what it might be like to be with Shane on a personal level? She had patients who needed her care and a funeral to plan for her stepfather. Not to mention trying to figure out who had tried to kidnap her and why.

Yeah, more than enough going on in her life at the moment. She pushed away from the door and quickly washed up before sitting on the bed to eat her salad. When she finished, she crawled into bed, despite the fact that it was barely nine o'clock at night.

It seemed as if she fell asleep the minute her head hit the pillow.

All too soon, the nightmare that had plagued her as a child returned. Deep in the recesses of her mind, she knew it was just a dream, but she couldn't seem to break loose.

Her father was working from home that day, sunshine streaming through his office windows. He hadn't minded her being there as long as she was quiet and didn't interrupt. Since she loved to read, that wasn't a problem and she was reading one of her old favorites, *The Black Stallion*, when the doorbell rang. Her father stood up and walked across the study just as there was a loud banging noise as someone burst in through the front door.

"Hide, Gabriella," her father whispered urgently. *"Under the desk. And don't make a sound! No matter what happens, don't let them see you!"*

She hadn't understood what was going on, but

she scrambled beneath the oak desk and covered her ears when the men started yelling.

Pain crushed her temples and suddenly, Shane was there, shaking her awake.

"Gabby, wake up! You're safe, Gabby. It's only a dream."

Her eyelids fluttered open and she realized the lamp was on and Shane was standing over her, holding on to her shoulders as if to keep her from thrashing around.

"What happened?" she asked in confusion, trying to throw off the effects of the nightmare. "Why are you here?"

"You were screaming," Shane said in a low, gravelly voice, his eyes full of concern. "You scared me to death, I thought for sure Creighton had found you."

She grimaced and put a hand to her head, trying to press the ache away. Now that he mentioned it, her throat hurt as if she'd spent the day shrieking at the top of her lungs. "Sorry," she murmured.

"I'll get you a cup of water," Shane said, releasing her shoulders and heading into the small bathroom.

She pushed herself up until she was sitting on the edge of the bed. She had to grasp the bedside table to keep herself steady.

"Here you go." Shane returned to her side and handed her a cup of water.

She was grateful for the arm he anchored around her shoulders. "Thanks," she murmured, taking a sip. "I'm sorry, but I might need my headache pills again. They're in my duffel."

He brought the pill bottle over and held her glass so she could take them. "You don't have to apologize, Gabby. I'm just glad you weren't in danger."

She couldn't suppress a shiver and did her best to push the last remnants of the nightmare away. "I haven't had this particular nightmare in a long time. Years, actually."

"But you've had this one before?" Shane asked with a puzzled frown. "What happened?"

She hesitated, reluctant to relive the painful past. "It's nothing, really. Just a memory of my father telling me to hide. And then nothing but angry voices and pain reverberating through my head."

"Your father told you to hide?" he echoed. "But you don't remember anything more? That seems odd, considering your amazing memory."

She closed her eyes for a moment, wishing she hadn't said anything at all. "I was eight," she reminded him. "And it hurts to think about it."

Shane knelt down in front of her so he could meet her gaze. "Gabby, don't you think it's strange that you get a headache every time you think about your father?" he asked in a gentle tone.

It took all her willpower not shut him out. "Of

course I think it's strange. My mother took me
to see a psychologist right after we moved, but
that didn't help. Besides, as I said before, what
difference does it make now? My father died
twenty-one years ago. Why on earth would any-
thing happening now be connected to something
that transpired way back then?"

"I don't know," Shane said. "I agree that it
doesn't seem likely that someone who might have
known your father had come back to find you
after all these years."

"Exactly," she said with a sigh.

"But, Gabby, I have to be honest with you,"
Shane continued, his expression grave. "These
terrible headaches of yours are troubling. I think
they're a sign of something serious, something
you shouldn't ignore."

She frowned, not liking what he was insinu-
ating. "You honestly want me to see a shrink?"

"I didn't say that. But don't you agree it's pos-
sible you may have repressed some painful mem-
ory? Something that's going to continue to cause
you headaches until you figure out what hap-
pened?"

She stared at him for a long minute. Deep
down, she knew he was right, although she des-
perately wished that he wasn't.

"I don't know," she whispered helplessly.
"Maybe. But do you really believe that my head-

aches have anything to do with what's going on now?"

"I don't think we can afford to assume that your past isn't connected to whatever is going on now," Shane said. "Maybe Creighton is linked to Richard's gambling debts. Or Creighton might be linked to Eric Ambrose, who certainly has a reason to search for the notes you kept during your residency. But will you promise me to at least think about it?" His gaze burned into her as he reached out and took her hand in his. "Please? For your own personal health as well as for your safety?"

She nodded, unable to refuse his request. Because he might be right. Not only would she be free of these infernal headaches, but maybe she needed to know what key her mind held about the past.

And she couldn't deny that not only was her safety important, but Shane's was, too. Because she was certain he'd do anything to protect her.

Which meant she needed to do her part in protecting him, too.

TEN

Shane slowly rose to his feet, relieved that Gabby had agreed to investigate the source of her headaches. His pulse still hadn't returned to normal after he'd woken to her heart-thundering scream.

It had taken him two frustrating attempts to get the combination numbers entered correctly, long seconds that had seemed to stretch forever. When he'd barreled inside, he'd been overwhelmingly relieved that she'd been alone and not held captive by some madman.

Although finding Gabby screaming, crying and covering her ears while in the throes of a horrible nightmare hadn't been a whole lot better.

He hated seeing her so deeply afraid.

Shane took a deep breath and let it out slowly. The hour was still early, barely four-thirty in the morning, so he headed for the door.

"Shane?"

He paused and turned back to face Gabby. "Yes?"

"Thank you for coming to my rescue."

"You're welcome," he said, forcing a smile. "Try to get some sleep, okay?"

Her answering smile was wry as she shook her head. "I'll try, but I doubt I'll be able to."

He hesitated, hating the idea of leaving her alone. "Is the cafeteria open this early? We could grab some coffee."

Gabby's expression brightened. "Are you sure you wouldn't mind? The cafeteria isn't open yet, but we could get some coffee from the ER and then head over to the cafeteria to sit down for a bit."

"I don't mind at all," he said, speaking the truth. He liked spending time with Gabby, far more than he should. Oh sure, he could tell himself he was playing bodyguard in order to safeguard her, but in reality he wanted to be there. The mere thought of handing over the job of protecting her to someone else didn't sit well, either.

"I'll, um, just grab my shoes," he said, glancing down at the pair of scrubs he'd used to sleep in. He needed to get a new uniform, but there should be time for that later.

"Okay, sounds good."

He left Gabby's call room and quickly pulled on his black cop boots, which looked ridiculous with his scrubs, so he took a few extra minutes to change back into his uniform. Not just because of the shoes, but because he didn't want to leave his weapon behind.

Just in case.

When he was fully dressed, he left the room, realizing that today was Sunday. His day off, unless a SWAT call came through.

Would Gabby be interested in attending church services with him?

He was surprised at how badly he wanted her to.

Shane returned next door to Gabby's room. "Ready?" she asked, looking better, as if she'd successfully put the remnants of her nightmare behind her.

He couldn't help but grin. "Absolutely."

Gabby led the way down the hall, past the rest of the call rooms. Shane glanced at room five, the one she'd used last night, frowning when he noticed the door to the room was ajar.

"Gabby, wait," he said, his voice rising with urgency. "Go back to your call room."

"What's wrong?" she asked, swinging around in alarm.

He pulled his weapon, keeping his gaze laser focused on the door. The odds of anyone still being inside were slim, but he didn't want to take any chances. Not with Gabby's life.

But room eleven was way down at the end of the hall, the exact path that an intruder might take to get away. On second thought, he decided she was better off staying here.

"Flatten yourself against the wall," he instructed in a hoarse whisper.

By now she'd noticed the open door, too, and thankfully did as he asked.

Shane pressed himself against the wall on the opposite side of the door before reaching out to shove the door open. It swung inward, and from his angle he could see the main part of the room appeared to be empty.

Ransacked, but still empty.

A chill snaked down his spine. The bed linens had been tossed on the floor, the mattress shoved partly off its corresponding box spring. The drawer to the small bedside table was upside down on the floor.

"Go back to your call room and contact Security," he ordered. Then he used the radio clipped to his label. "Dispatch, this is unit twelve. Potential intruder at Trinity Medical Center, location in question is call room number five situated behind the ER. I need officer backup ASAP."

Gabby's eyes widened and this time, instead of balking, she edged around him and then ran down the hall to her call room. He couldn't deny a flash of relief when he watched her punch the buttons for the code and then disappear inside.

Shane debated waiting for backup, since he felt certain the intruder who'd done this was long gone.

But the small bathroom was located on the far

wall, behind the door. There was a remote possibility that the intruder was still in there, hiding.

Lying in wait.

Shane couldn't imagine why the perp would stick around, unless he planned on making another attempt to kidnap Gabby. But then why leave a mess behind as an early warning?

No, the more he turned the idea over in his mind, the more convinced he became that the call room was empty. He'd wait for backup because there was no sense in getting on Griff's bad side again.

One of the hospital security guards arrived, a young guy who appeared about thirty pounds overweight, his chest heaving from exertion. "I'm the senior officer on night shift. Someone hiding in there?" he asked between panting breaths.

"Doubtful, but I'm waiting for backup to make sure. In the meantime, I need you to stand guard outside call room number ten. Dr. Fielding is in there."

"Got it," the security officer said, hurrying farther down the hall.

A security officer armed with nothing more than a Taser wasn't exactly reassuring, but at least the young man seemed to take his job seriously.

Feeling impatient, Shane called Dispatch

again. "This is officer twelve, what's the status on backup?"

"Entering the ER now, should be there in a few minutes," the dispatcher said calmly.

"Ten-four." Shane tightened his grip on his weapon, keeping his eye on the call room. A young third-shift deputy by the name of Jay Sanford arrived less than a minute later.

"The room has been tossed," he told Jay. "Dr. Fielding used this room last night, so I believe the perp assumed she was still here. I doubt he decided to hang around, but we need to be sure. The bathroom is located on the far wall, across from the bed. I'll go in first."

Jay nodded. "I'm ready."

Shane ducked into the room, first verifying there was no one behind the door.

The bathroom door remained shut and he crept forward, keeping up against the wall. Bullets could go through flimsy doors and drywall without a problem.

He twisted the door handle, glad it wasn't locked. When he pushed the door open, he was stunned to see a guy in scrubs lying with his hands tied behind his back and a rag tied over his mouth, apparently unconscious on the floor. Shane dropped to his knees, feeling for a pulse, thankfully finding one.

"Get Gabby in here right away," he shouted to Jay. "Room ten, go!"

The man on the floor groaned as Shane pulled out his pocketknife to cut through his bindings. As he was removing the gag, Gabby arrived.

"Oh, no," she cried, dropping down beside the prone figure. "We need to get help from the ER."

"I'll go," the security officer volunteered.

"Do you know him?" Shane asked Gabby as she carefully eased the man over on his back.

She nodded, her expression grim. "Brandon Johnson, one of our trauma attending physicians. Did Creighton do this?"

Shane sighed. "I believe so. After all, this was the room you were using until late last night."

"It doesn't make sense," Gabby muttered. "How could he find out the combination on the door? Even if he did come in to search the room, why would he stick around to wait?"

"He was probably expecting you, Gabby," Shane said slowly. "And if that's the case, it's just sheer luck on our part that we moved several call rooms down."

"Poor Steve," she whispered brokenly. "He was hurt and it's all my fault."

"Not your fault—*Creighton's*," Shane reminded her.

"I can't stay here," Gabby said in a hushed tone, her tortured gaze meeting his. "I have to take a leave of absence from work. I can't keep putting my colleagues at risk."

"I know," Shane murmured. "I'm sorry, Gabby."

At that moment the security guard arrived, bringing an ER doctor, a nurse and a gurney.

Gabby insisted on helping as they rolled the physician onto a long board. There wasn't a lot of room in the tiny bathroom, but somehow they managed to use the long board to lift him up and carry him out to the waiting gurney.

"I'm sorry, I'm so sorry," Gabby repeated helplessly.

"We'll take good care of him," the ER doctor assured her before they whisked Brandon away.

Gabby stood in the hallway, staring after the retreating gurney, looking completely shell-shocked.

"Don't do this, Gabby," he said in a gruff tone. "It's not your fault."

"Yes, it is. I should have anticipated something like this. After all, you told me I needed to move to a different room. I should have told the operator to keep this room vacant. If something happens to Brandon…" Her voice trailed off.

He wrapped his arm around her slim shoulders and drew her close. "He's going to be okay. Creighton didn't shoot him, which makes me think that this guy might have caught him by surprise."

For an instant Gabby leaned against him, as if suddenly weary. Then she abruptly straightened. "We need to get out of here before anything else happens."

He nodded, glancing over at Jay. "I'd like a crime scene tech to go through the room, just in case."

"On it," Jay agreed.

"I'm taking her someplace safe, and then I'll be in touch." Shane took Gabby's arm and escorted her back to her room. He waited patiently in the hallway while she gathered her things.

Gabby believed she was responsible for Brandon's injury, but Shane knew the blame rested squarely on his own shoulders.

Regret coursed through him. He'd allowed himself to be complacent…to believe that Gabby was better off in a familiar place surrounded by people who knew her and cared about her.

Yet Creighton had almost found her, anyway.

Close. The whole thing had been too close. And an innocent bystander had gotten hurt as a result.

No way could he afford to make a mistake in judgment like that again.

Gabby blinked back tears, trying to get the vision of Brandon's unconscious body out of her mind as she changed from her scrubs. She drew on her favorite pair of black stretch pants topped with a green sweater. Tossing her things back into her duffel bag didn't take long, and she soon emerged from the call room. "Let's go," she said to Shane, anxious to leave before something else happened.

Gabby desperately wanted to know how Brandon was doing, but she knew it would take time to get him examined and then sent to Radiology for testing. Even then, the results from the CT scan wouldn't be back for at least twenty minutes.

And she planned to be long gone from the hospital by then.

"This way," Shane instructed, taking her duffel from her and slinging it over his shoulder. He took the back stairs down to the outside exit.

He didn't rush but seemed to be keeping a sharp lookout as they went. When the stairwell ended in a doorway leading outside, she sucked in a harsh breath at the chill in the air.

Shane put out his arm, holding her back for a long moment before moving forward and taking the sidewalk around the building to the parking structure.

She soon realized that this could very well be the exact path Creighton had used after knocking out Brandon and tying him up.

It wasn't easy to swallow past the lump in her throat. And she didn't once look back at the brightly lit hospital as she followed Shane to his police vehicle.

"Are you all right?" he asked once they were both inside the car.

She shrugged, looking away from his probing glance. "As good as I can be."

Shane didn't press the issue, but he did reach out to take her hand in his, giving it a gentle squeeze. Oddly enough, the sweet gesture made tears prick behind her eyes again.

She subtly wiped them away as Shane drove out of the structure and headed toward the interstate. There wasn't much traffic at five-thirty in the morning, so it didn't take long to hit the open road.

"Where are we going?" she finally asked.

"There's a motel called the American Lodge that happens to be located not far from my church. I'll get us connecting rooms there."

Swiveling toward him, she studied his strong, masculine profile as he expertly maneuvered the multilane freeway. "Do you live near there, too?"

"No, my place is a few miles in the opposite direction. But right now we're not going to the motel. We're meeting Nate to swap this ride for something else."

"A different car? Why?"

He glanced over at her, his expression grim. "I have to assume that Creighton knows who I am. He must have seen me sleeping outside call room number five, otherwise there is no way he could have figured out which room you were in."

It took a minute for that information to sink in. "You think he had the nerve to follow us inside the hospital? And that he seriously knows who you are?"

"Yeah," Shane said. "Unfortunately, I do. So we need a vehicle that can't be linked to either one of us."

Gabby tried to swallow another wave of guilt. Who had hired Creighton to do all of this? And why?

"I'm sorry," she whispered.

"Hey, you don't have to apologize, Gabby." Shane reached over once again to take her hand. "This is Creighton's fault, not yours. He hurt Brandon, not you. We're going to get to the bottom of this…you'll see."

She wanted, desperately, to believe him. But it wasn't easy. She closed her eyes and thought about how Shane had prayed with her over her stepfather's bedside. Gabby had expected to feel awkward but had been pleasantly surprised to experience a sense of peace instead.

Maybe she could try that again. Granted, she didn't have much experience, but she tried to clear her mind and focus on the prayer.

Dear Lord, please heal Brandon's injuries and keep me and Shane safe in Your care. Amen.

She took a deep breath and opened her eyes. Shane squeezed her hand and she glanced at him in surprise.

"Gabby, would you please attend church with

me today? There's a ten o'clock service that we should be able to make in plenty of time."

"I'd like that," she agreed, touched by his offer. She tried to tell herself not to make a big deal out of his invitation, but it wasn't easy. She knew Shane probably didn't want to skip the service, so of course he'd ask her to go along rather than leave her alone in a motel room.

Still, the satisfied expression on his handsome face made her wonder if Shane might actually want her to be with him on a personal level. Oddly enough, she found she liked the idea of being more to him than just another responsibility.

He exited the freeway and then turned to head south. Soon he pulled into the driveway of a chain restaurant that specialized in making breakfast.

"I hope you're hungry, because I guarantee Nate is going to order breakfast."

Her stomach growled with anticipation. "I am," she confessed.

They headed inside the restaurant and she easily caught sight of Nate seated in a booth along the north wall. He waved them over.

Gabby took the seat across from him, hyperaware of Shane as he slid in beside her. Their server hurried over holding a pot of black coffee.

"Yes, please," Gabby said gratefully as she pushed her cup over.

Their server filled up their mugs and then handed out menus. "I'll be back in a few minutes to take your order."

Gabby added a liberal dose of cream to her mug before taking a sip.

"Did you bring me a different set of wheels?" Shane asked.

"Yep." Nate slid a key fob across the table. "Don't be upset, it's a nine-year-old car that my aunt Margaret agreed to let me borrow for a few days."

"Thanks," Shane said, taking the keys. "Did you bring clothes for me, too?"

"In the car," his buddy confirmed.

Gabby watched Nate warily, wondering if he still believed the worst about her. The way he'd interrogated her during that so-called interview still rankled.

She lowered her gaze to the menu, determined not to let Nate's suspicions ruin her appetite.

"Thanks," Shane said. "Be careful driving my car back to headquarters. I have to believe Creighton saw me outside Gabby's call room, and if he knows who I am, then it's highly likely he has the license plate number of my vehicle, too."

"I can handle it," Nate assured him. "I've convinced Griff to put your vehicle through its annual maintenance check a few months early. That way no one else will be driving it, either."

"Good. That's good." Shane glanced down at

his menu. "I'm hungry. I think I'll have the full Irish breakfast."

"Me, too," Nate agreed. For the first time since she sat down, he looked at her directly. "Are you ready to order?"

"Yes. I'll have the breakfast special." She closed her menu just as their server returned.

When they were alone once again, Nate eyed her over the brim of his coffee mug. "I have some interesting information."

Tiny alarm bells went off in the back of her mind.

"What?" Shane demanded, leaning across the table toward him. "Did you find Eric Ambrose?"

Nate grimaced. "Not yet. We're still looking though. The information I have is on Gabby's father, Travis Fielding."

The knot in her stomach tightened and the headache that she'd pushed out of the way after her nightmare came back with a vengeance.

"Gabby, did you know your father was a certified public accountant?"

She frowned. "Yes, so what?"

"Apparently he worked for one of the largest casinos in Las Vegas before he allegedly died of a heart attack. But here's the thing. Why would you and your mother be taken into witness protection after your father's death if he only died of a heart attack? I'm not buying it. I think it's more likely that your father was involved in something illegal."

The pounding in her temples intensified, but since she was blocked in the booth by Shane, there was no way to flee.

To escape.

She knew Shane and Nate wanted to know what she remembered, but that was the problem. She didn't remember anything related to her father's death.

Obviously, Shane was right. She needed to find a way to get past the headaches to find the truth.

Before it was too late.

ELEVEN

Shane glanced at Gabby, wishing there was something he could do to erase the pinched expression on her face.

To ease the shadow of pain in her luminous green eyes.

But he also couldn't ignore the truth in Nate's words. It was likely that Travis Fielding had been involved in something illegal, otherwise there would have been no reason to place Gabby and her mother in witness protection.

But why would anyone wait twenty-one years to come after her? It still didn't make sense.

"I don't know what you want me to say," Gabby whispered, pressing her fingertips against the sides of her temples. "I don't remember anything other than what I've already told you."

"It's okay," Shane murmured, putting his arm protectively around her shoulders and ignoring Nate's pointed gaze. He understood his buddy was suspicious, but there was no way Gabby was faking these headaches.

"I need to use the restroom," she whispered again.

Shane didn't want Gabby to be alone, but there wasn't much he could do to stop her from leaving. And maybe she needed a few minutes to pull herself together. He slid out of the booth, allowing her room to get out. When Gabby headed toward the restrooms, he slid back in and glared at Nate.

"What's your problem?" he demanded. "Why do you believe she's involved in this?"

"*You're* the problem," Nate accused. "You're too emotionally involved with her. She was kidnapped at gunpoint, wasn't she? Therefore she's involved."

Shane suppressed a sigh. "Yeah, but she's the victim. This isn't like you, Nate. You're normally a huge advocate for victims. What's really going on?"

Nate paused for a moment and shrugged. "Okay, fine. You want to know what's going on? I'm worried about you. Right from the beginning you've been on her side. You're the new guy on the team and I want to be sure you're looking at this investigation through impartial eyes."

Shane conceded that Nate had a point. "All right, I can appreciate that. But you have to trust me on this. Gabby is a victim. She's dedicated her life to saving trauma patients. Why would she throw all of that away on something illegal?"

"I don't know," Nate admitted.

"She wouldn't," Shane said firmly. "Gabby suffered through a difficult childhood and still managed to come out on top. She paid her step-father's mortgage because of a deathbed promise to her mother. I'm telling you, she has too much integrity to be involved in something illegal."

A faint smile flashed across Nate's features. "But you're not too personally invested in her, right?"

Touché, Shane thought wryly. "I care about her as someone who needs protection, nothing more. I'm dedicated to keeping her safe until we get Creighton or whoever hired him behind bars."

"So this isn't the same way you were dedicated to helping your former fiancée, Linda? The same woman who later walked away, stating that she'd mistaken her tender feelings toward you for love, when in fact she was just grateful for your help."

His mouth tightened. "She did more than walk away, she *cheated* on me."

"Yeah, but that was only because she didn't really love you. She appreciated your protection, but being grateful isn't being in love."

Shane dropped his gaze to stare into his coffee mug. "Linda was a cop, just like me. She didn't need protection, not the same way Gabby does."

"But she was in an abusive relationship, wasn't

she?" his friend pressed. "And you can't deny you were helping to keep her safe from her ex-boyfriend."

No, he couldn't deny it. But no matter what Nate thought, he wasn't making the same mistake with Gabby.

Deep down Shane knew that there couldn't be anything more than friendship between them. Had been telling himself that from the beginning, the night she was kidnapped right before his eyes.

So why had he kissed her?

Shane shoved a hand through his hair. Truthfully? He had no idea. But as wonderful as it had been to feel his lips brush against hers, he absolutely couldn't do that again. He needed to remember that as soon as they found Creighton, he and Gabby would go their separate ways.

Because Nate was right. Gratitude was a poor substitute for love.

Gabby walked back out to the table just as their server was bringing breakfast. The concerned expression in Shane's intense blue eyes warmed her heart. At least he believed in her.

Shane scooted over to give her room. Then he bowed his head for a moment and silently prayed. She noticed Nate waited for him to finish, the same way she did, before digging into his food.

Her appetite had waned beneath the weight of her headache, but she forced herself to try to eat.

"I wish we could find Ambrose," Shane muttered darkly. "The timing of Gabby's kidnapping in conjunction with the lawsuit is suspicious. I can't help thinking he might be the one behind all this."

Nate nodded. "You could be right. And we *are* trying to find him. I've asked both the Illinois state troopers and the Chicago PD to be on alert, but so far we haven't heard anything."

"Gabby, would you mind sharing those notes you kept related to Ambrose and Chasco?" Shane asked.

"No, I don't mind," she agreed warily, even though she didn't particularly want to read through them again. "But I don't know that they'll be any help since the events happened four years ago. Besides, the notes are in a safe-deposit box that we won't be able to access until tomorrow."

"All right, maybe we can do that in the morning, as soon as the banks open." Shane reached over to pour ketchup on his hash browns. "Maybe they won't help, but reviewing them might give us a better picture of Ambrose."

She didn't necessarily agree but wouldn't stand in Shane's way, either. Silence fell as the guys concentrated on their breakfast while she picked at her food.

Their server came back to refill their coffee mugs and to set the bill on the table. Nate picked it up and reached for his wallet.

"I can get it," Shane protested.

"Nope. No paper trail with your name on it," the other man said firmly. "I'll give you whatever cash I have on hand, too."

Gabby glanced up at Nate, who was regarding her steadily. "Thank you," she said in a quiet tone. "I appreciate everything you're doing for me."

There was a pause before Nate inclined his head. "You're welcome."

"Are you finished?" Shane frowned at her half-eaten food.

"Almost." She did her best to eat as much as possible before pushing her plate away.

Nate gave them the make and model of his aunt's car before he walked over to the cashier to pay the bill. Shane rested his hand on the small of her back as they walked outside.

"That must be it," he said, steering her toward an older-model sedan. Nate's aunt must take good care of her cars, because there wasn't a speck of rust on the body, despite the vehicle's age.

Shane glanced at his watch. "We have about an hour and a half until church starts. How about we see if we can secure the motel rooms? I know it's early, but it's worth a shot."

"All right," she agreed. Gabby folded her hands

in her lap, not sure what to expect from going to church services with Shane. Normally she avoided listening to people preaching at her. But then again, she found it difficult to believe Shane would like something like that, too.

She rested against the seat cushions as he drove. Closing her eyes and doing her deep-breathing exercises helped to ease her headache. When she opened her eyes, she was surprised to discover that thirty minutes had passed.

"This is it," Shane said, gesturing to the motel on the left-hand side of the road.

Beyond the motel, she could see a white church steeple rising above the trees rippling with red, orange, yellow and green leaves. Autumn was her favorite time of year.

Shane pulled into the small carport in front of the hotel lobby. They walked inside, Shane an impressive sight in his black SWAT uniform.

"I need connecting rooms, please," he told the woman behind the counter. "Preferably on the ground floor."

The woman checked her computer. "I do have connecting rooms available but check-in time is normally at three o'clock in the afternoon."

"I understand, but couldn't you make an exception if the rooms are already vacant?" Shane pressed.

The woman glanced at his badge and then nodded. "Sure, I guess so."

Shane smiled. "Thanks," he said and she no-
ticed he slipped her an extra twenty. "I'd also
like to pay with cash, please."

The woman insisted on checking his ID, but
Gabby was surprised she'd agreed to his paying
with cash. Amazing what a good-looking man
in a cop uniform could get you.

Ten minutes later, she dropped her duffel bag
on the bed and glanced curiously around the
room. Nothing special, but it was clean, so she
had no right to complain.

Gabby unpacked her bag, wondering if she
should change for church or not. Her black
stretch pants and green sweater were more ca-
sual, but surely better than jeans.

She drew the cedar box out of her bag. A light
rap on the connecting door startled her enough
that she almost dropped it. She carefully set the
box on the bedside table before crossing over and
opening the door.

Shane stood there, still wearing his uniform.
"Hi. I'm going to take a quick shower, and then
we can walk over to church, okay?"

"Sure," she agreed. "Am I dressed all right?"

He smiled reassuringly. "You're perfect. Nate
provided me jeans and a sweater, so I'll be more
casual than you are. Just give me ten to fifteen
minutes, all right?"

"Of course." She left the door ajar and then
went back to unpacking. She needed to call her

boss, Jonathan Murray, chief of trauma surgery, to let him know she needed some time off work. She picked up the motel phone but then replaced it.

Maybe it would be better to use Shane's phone to make the call since she also needed to find out how Brandon was doing.

Remaining patient wasn't easy, and soon she found herself pacing the width of the motel room. How was she going to manage being off work for any length of time? Would Shane allow her to go out for a run after church? Watching television was of no interest, and she hadn't brought her latest murder mystery to read.

Shane knocked again on the connecting door and then pushed it open. He looked absolutely amazing in his cable-knit sweater and black jeans, his face freshly shaved and his dark hair still damp from his shower.

For a moment she stared at him, her tongue seemingly glued to the top of her mouth. What was wrong with her? She'd seen plenty of handsome men before. Several of the physicians she worked with were good-looking.

But there was only one Shane Hawkins.

"Ready to go?" he asked.

She managed to nod in agreement and hoped he didn't notice her warm face. When they walked outside, Shane reached for her hand and she didn't pull away, even though she knew she should.

The walk to church didn't take long, and for some reason most of her anxiety about attending services seemed to vanish as they approached the pretty white church with the beautiful stained-glass windows. Everyone was so friendly, calling out greetings as they walked up to the door.

"Shane!" His sister, Leah, waved at them from a pew near the front of the church and Gabby could see that Isaac and Ben were there, too. Shane tugged her forward, obviously intending to join them.

"Gabby, it's so good to see you!" Leah gave her a quick hug. "You remember my husband, Isaac? And my son, Ben?"

"Yes, of course." She shook Isaac's hand and smiled when Shane lifted Ben up to give him a hug. When he set Ben back down on his feet, he greeted Isaac like a brother. Of course, they were brothers by marriage, but there was obviously a deep friendship between the two men as well.

Somehow, she found herself sandwiched between Leah and Shane as the choir began to sing. Gabby let the music wash over her, filling her with a wonderful sense of peace. Listening to the words of the opening hymn, she couldn't deny feeling a sense of belonging, and not just because she was standing here with friends. But because she was surrounded by people who believed in God.

She couldn't help wondering what her childhood would have been like if she'd been exposed to church and faith. Granted, it wouldn't have changed the way her stepfather had treated her, or the environment she'd lived in at boarding school, but she doubted she would have felt so alone.

With Mary Jane Pollard as her only ally.

The theme of the pastor's sermon was faithfulness, and one particular passage from Psalms struck a chord, resonating deep within.

Do not withhold your mercy from me, Lord; may Your love and faithfulness always protect me (Psalm 40:11).

The thought of having God's love with her at all times was humbling. When it came time to recite the Lord's Prayer, she was finally able to let go of the resentment she'd been holding against Richard. She found herself hoping that her stepfather would rest in peace.

She tried, really tried, to release the anger she harbored toward Damon, but couldn't quite let it go. She felt bad about that, and hoped that over time she'd grow better at praying and following God's word.

When the final hymn was over, she reluctantly followed Shane out of the church, knowing deep in her heart that she'd like nothing better than to return for services next Sunday.

"So how are things going, Gabby?" Leah

asked when they made it outside. "I know it's been crazy busy at work."

For the first time in a long time, her job wasn't in the forefront of her mind. "Yes, it's been busy," she agreed. "But I'm off for the next few days, so hopefully I'll be refreshed by the time I go back."

"Any big plans?" Shane's sister asked, her curious gaze bouncing between Gabby and Shane.

"No special plans," she assured her. And, thankfully, Leah didn't ask anything more.

"Uncle Shane, don't you want to come to Toyland with us?" Ben asked.

"Maybe next time, buddy," Shane said, ruffling Ben's hair. "Have fun with your mom and dad, okay?"

"Okay." The little boy waved and then ran after Leah and Isaac as they walked back to their car.

"Let's walk in the opposite direction for a bit," Shane suggested. "I'd rather not let anyone know that we're staying at the motel down the street."

"All right," she agreed, understanding where he was coming from. "Thank you for bringing me along," she added softly as they strolled down the street. "I enjoyed the service."

"Really?" The frank hope in Shane's deep masculine tone surprised her. "You're not just saying that?"

She smiled and shook her head. "I have to say that I wasn't sure what to expect. And I was able to let go of my resentment toward Richard. Now, if only I could do that with—" She abruptly cut herself off, embarrassed to realize she'd been about to tell Shane about Damon.

"Do that with what?" Shane asked gently.

She swallowed hard, wishing she'd guarded her tongue. "It's nothing."

"Okay, but I'm here if you want to talk," Shane said. "And sometimes secrets can fester if they're kept buried too long."

Gabby sighed, hating it when he was right. But this was more than just a secret. It was a betrayal that had shattered her innocence.

And even though she knew she wasn't to blame, she couldn't seem to forget Damon's parting accusation about how she'd been asking for it.

"Gabby?" The husky tone of Shane's voice broke through the memory.

"Remember that boyfriend I had in my first year as a resident?" she whispered. "His name was Damon Keller and, as you know, things didn't end well between us."

Shane's pace slowed to the point they were hardly moving. "I remember you said you broke things off with him," he agreed, his eyes darkening with concern. "Did something happen? Did he cheat on you the same way my fiancée cheated on me?"

She wished it were that simple. Not that she was making light of what Shane had been through. Linda had made a commitment to marry him; she had no business cheating on Shane behind his back.

Truth was, both of them were better off without the Lindas and Damons of the world.

"Damon and I used to study together, shared lunch in the cafeteria together. When he invited me to his place for pizza and a movie, I didn't think twice about going."

Shane stopped beneath the shade of a large maple tree and took both of her hands in his. "Gabby? What happened?"

She couldn't meet his gaze. "Well, he never intended to watch a movie, that's for sure."

Shane's arms filled with tension, but his grasp on her hands remained gentle. "Did he hurt you?"

She nodded. "He pinned me on the couch, kept kissing me, grabbing me. I was so shocked…so afraid."

"Gabby…" Ironically, the tortured sound of Shane's voice gave her the strength to tell him the rest.

"I hit him in the face, stunned him long enough to get away before he could finish. I ran out of his apartment, sobbing and holding together my torn blouse while he screamed at me that it was all my fault, that I was asking for it."

"Oh, Gabby…" Shane pulled her into his arms, holding her gently against his chest. "I hope you went to the police and pressed assault charges against him."

"No," she said, her voice muffled against his sweater. "I didn't. Because, deep down, I believed he might be right."

"Not true," Shane bit out. "No means no, and that's the end of it. Date rape is all too common, and almost always goes unreported."

Gabby lifted her head to meet Shane's fierce blue gaze. "That's not really what I meant. *Of course* I wasn't asking to be assaulted. But I was young, barely twenty, with absolutely no experience with men. Maybe other women understood some unspoken rule that if you went to a guy's apartment you were pretty much agreeing to be intimate. But I didn't know."

"Wrong again," Shane said harshly. "None of that matters, Gabby. He's the one who didn't listen when you said no and he's the one who tried to blame you for his actions."

The way Shane defended her was so sweet, she just had to smile. "You're amazing," she said huskily. "Thank you for making me feel better. And maybe one day I'll be able to forgive him."

Shane stared at her for a long moment. "Gabby, last night when I kissed you, I didn't mean—"

"Don't, Shane," she interrupted him. "Your kiss was wonderful. My reaction was because of Damon not you." She hesitated and then asked, "Actually, I was hoping we could try that again."

"What?" Shane looked dumbfounded.

When he didn't move, she slowly raised up on her tiptoes and tentatively pressed her mouth against his. Shane held her carefully, allowing her to have control of the kiss.

And when he tenderly kissed her back, she wrapped her arms around his neck and melted into his embrace.

TWELVE

Shane kept his kiss light and gentle, refusing to do anything that might make Gabby feel afraid. When she wrapped her arms around his neck, he had to remind himself to maintain control, no easy feat, considering the way her citrusy scent was wreaking havoc with his senses.

Her lips teased his and he cautiously allowed her to deepen the kiss, hoping, praying she wouldn't regret this. His pulse leaped in response and he desperately wanted to pull her close but didn't move, allowing Gabby to explore within her own comfort zone.

When she finally broke off the kiss and smiled shyly up at him, he was overwhelmed with relief. She'd taken the first step and, hopefully, from here on out, she'd be okay.

"Thanks," she murmured softly.

He took a moment to pull his scattered brain cells into some semblance of order. "Gabby, I'm always here for you, no matter what."

She loosened her grip around his neck but didn't let go. Shane liked the fact that she felt comfortable being so close to him. She tipped her head to the side, regarding him steadily. Her green sweater heightened the color of her eyes, and the way her red curls framed her face made her so beautiful, she literally took his breath away.

"I didn't know kisses could be so special," she whispered. "Or maybe it's just you."

Yes! he wanted to shout at the top of his lungs. Because no way did he like the idea of Gabby practicing kisses with another man. But he held his tongue because past experience had taught him that what Gabby was feeling toward him right now wasn't real. She was in a dangerous and vulnerable situation, completely out of her element. She was leaning on him because he was there, protecting her.

As soon as the danger was over and they'd captured Creighton, or whoever hired him, this close association would end. She had her life and he had his. She'd soon realize that there were other men out there, men she might be attracted to. After all, hadn't he seen with his own eyes that she was surrounded by doctors? Physicians she may not have noticed before because of what that jerk had done to her? Highly likely that Gabby might now be able to come out of her protective shell to see the men she worked with differently. Every fiber of his being rebelled at the idea, but he forced himself not to show his turbulent feelings.

No way could he afford to repeat the mistakes of his past.

"Shane?" Gabby said his name in a low, hesitant tone. "Is something wrong?"

He forced himself to smile. "Nothing is wrong, Gabby," he said huskily. "I'm happy that you've begun to put your fears behind you. I hate that you had to suffer at a man's hands in the first place." If the statute of limitations hadn't run out, he'd head out to arrest the guy.

Gabby's own smile dimmed and he caught a glimpse of disappointment reflected in her eyes.

He sighed and reached over to tuck a stray curl behind her ear. "Gabby, we've been thrown together in the heat of danger, and it's not unusual for emotions to become more intense in these types of situations. I care about you, and I'll do everything in my power to keep you safe. But right now, we can't afford to lose focus regarding the fact that someone is still trying to get to you."

Her gaze clung to his for a long moment before she nodded and drew away, stepping back and crossing her arms over her chest. The moment she released him, he balled his fingers into fists so he wouldn't reach out and pull her close again.

He missed the warmth of her sweet embrace.

"I guess we should head back to the motel," she said, changing the subject.

From their position under the tree, he could see that the area around the church had thinned dramatically. Most of the parishioners had left or were walking toward their cars. "Sure, we'll go there now," he agreed.

"Tell me about Linda," Gabby said as they strolled casually along the road in the direction of the church, since the motel was just a mile farther. "How did you meet her?"

He wasn't sure why she was suddenly curious about his former fiancée, but since she'd been honest with him, he owed her the same frankness. "We worked together, she was a cop within my district."

"A cop?" She glanced up at him in surprise. "Were you partners?"

"No, not partners. But she was in a tough situation, her ex-boyfriend had a temper and had hit her a few times. She discovered he was stalking her, so I helped her put together a case against him."

"I see," Gabby murmured. "That explains it," she added.

He frowned. "Explains what?"

"Why you think that the feelings that are building between us aren't real," she stated in a matter-of-fact tone. "You rescued her, and she began to lean on you. But in the end, her feelings weren't real, they were a result of a heightened awareness that comes from being in danger."

Shane shouldn't have been surprised by her astute insight to his failed relationship. "Yes," he admitted quietly.

"And now you think I'm doing the same thing your ex-fiancée did," she went on.

He hesitated, not sure how to respond to that. He didn't *think* she was doing the same thing— he was absolutely certain she was.

But Gabby didn't realize that's what she was doing. Not yet. The same way Linda hadn't, until she began to fall in love for real.

"Not exactly," he said, choosing his words carefully. His phone rang, saving him from needing to come up with some way to smooth things over. He pulled out his phone, tipping the screen so Gabby could see Nate's name across the top. "Hey, Nate, what's up?"

"Chicago PD called to let us know they believe Eric Ambrose is in the area," Nate said. "Unfortunately, they lost him, but hopefully they'll find him soon."

"How could they lose him?" Shane asked in exasperation.

"I know, but the cop who was driving past Joe Chasco's place called in Ambrose's license plates, but before he could stop, he was notified about a shooting located a few miles away, so he had to leave."

"So Ambrose did go to Chicago to be with Chasco," Shane muttered, glancing at Gabby, who was listening intently. "Our instincts were right on."

"Yeah, it would be nice to have a break in the case," Nate agreed. "I'll keep in touch."

"Thanks." Shane disconnected from the call and then glanced down at his phone, making a mental note to swap it out as soon as possible. Just in case whoever this Creighton guy was had the ability to track his cell phone.

"I can't believe Eric is really in Chicago," Gabby croaked. "Even though I knew that he was a suspect, deep down I didn't really believe it."

"I'm sorry, Gabby," he said, picking up his pace. Knowing Ambrose was nearby was enough to make him want to get her back to the relative safety of the motel. He also took the battery out of his phone as an extra precaution, tucking it in the back pocket of his jeans.

"You and me, both," Gabby said with a grimace. "I hope Eric comes to his senses, before it's too late."

Grimacing, Shane slid a glance her way. The sooner they managed to get Ambrose into custody, the better. Because as much as he knew that Gabby's feelings toward him were heightened by the very real danger she faced, he couldn't necessarily say the same thing about his feelings for her.

Despite not wanting to make the same mistakes he'd made with Linda, he was very afraid it was too late. He cared about Gabby—too much for his peace of mind.

Gabby tried to hide her disappointment as she walked beside Shane up to their motel room. The kiss they'd shared, being held in his arms, had been amazing.

Shane could tell himself that her feelings weren't real, but she knew the truth. She cared about him.

A lot.

When he put a hand on her arm, preventing her from unlocking her motel room door, she looked up at him in surprise.

"Me first," he said. "Just to be safe."

She stared at him, wondering if he really believed that Creighton or Ambrose had found them there. Or maybe he was trying to remind her that he was there only for her protection, nothing more. Feeling oddly bereft, she handed him the key and moved off to the side. Shane used her key to open the door. He pushed the door open with his foot, keeping his hands free even though he wasn't armed, since he obviously hadn't carried his weapon with him to church.

She peered inside, seeing for herself the room was empty. He cautiously stepped inside and made his way to the tiny bathroom. A few minutes later, he returned and then went through the connecting door between their rooms.

Less than two minutes later, he returned to the doorway. "All clear," he said as he hooked his gun holster onto his belt.

Gabby nodded, wondering just what he had expected. "I'd like to call the hospital now, to check on Brandon's condition," she murmured. "Is it safe to use this phone here?"

Shane hesitated but then nodded. "I would think so... I can't imagine Creighton has access to your hospital phone records."

"Good." She used the phone to make the local call, relieved when the ER nurse reassured her that Brandon was fine.

"He's awake, has a minor concussion but otherwise seems to be okay," the nurse assured her. "They're talking about keeping him overnight for observation."

For a moment, the image of Richard flashed into her mind. "Who's the attending on duty?" she asked abruptly.

"Dr. Sebastian, why?"

"I need to talk to him right away," she said, not bothering to hide the urgency in her tone.

"Okay." After a few moments of silence, she could hear Sebastian's deep baritone over the line.

"Gabby? What's wrong?"

"How bad is Brandon's concussion?" she asked. "Does he really need to stay overnight?"

"His CT scan is normal. I was thinking of sending him home, but apparently his wife is out of town, so there isn't anyone to watch over him."

Gabby closed her eyes and pinched the bridge of her nose. "Listen, I'm worried that whoever hit Brandon in the first place might try to come after him again. If he has to stay, do me a favor and put him under an alias name. Just in case."

"Gabby, what's going on?" Sebastian demanded. "First, you're suddenly on a leave of absence, and now someone intentionally hurt Brandon?"

"I know it's my fault—I'm sorry. Please use the alias name, all right?"

"I will," Sebastian replied grudgingly.

Gabby hung up the phone and turned to see Shane standing close behind her. The urge to throw herself into his arms was overwhelming.

"Alias name?" he repeated with admiration in his tone. "Wow, that's brilliant. I'm sure that will keep him safe."

Gabby bit her lower lip. "I should have requested that for Richard," she said in a low voice.

"There's no reason to think your stepfather's death was the result of foul play," Shane said firmly. "Didn't that doctor friend of yours mention a blood clot?"

She nodded since he was right about Bill's theory.

"All right then, stop beating yourself up over this."

"I'll try." She glanced around the motel room with a sense of helpless frustration. "So now what? I need something to do or I'll go crazy."

"I know what you mean," Shane said wryly. "What if we go for a drive? I've been thinking we should pick up a few burner cell phones to use."

Burner phones? For a moment the conversation seemed surreal. She didn't live in this world of looking for bad guys around every corner, using cash and burner phones to hide their electronic trail.

Was Shane right about situations like these causing intense emotions? Feelings that might not last?

She didn't want to admit it, but he was probably right. Her world had been knocked off-kilter from the moment those men had taken her hostage at gunpoint.

Since he was watching her intently, waiting for a response to his question, she nodded. "Sure, why not? Anything to get out of this motel room for a while."

She followed Shane out into the bright sunlight as they walked to Nate's aunt's car.

He stayed on the side roads as he drove to a well-known big-box store. She was oddly surprised that purchasing the two disposable phones didn't take long, and soon they were back on the road.

"Here, we're going to need my phone to get those activated," Shane said, handing her his cell phone. She put the battery back in and waited a few minutes for the device to power up.

Before she could use it, though, it rang, displaying Nate's name and number across the screen. Shane was driving, so she answered. "Yes?"

"Gabby? Where's Shane?"

"Hang on, he's right here." She handed the phone to Shane. "It's Nate."

"Put it on speaker," Shane instructed.

She did as he asked and held the phone between them.

"I've been trying to call you," Nate accused. "We have a lead on Ambrose."

"I had the phone off," Shane admitted. "Where is he? Does the Chicago PD have him in custody?"

"No, but he crossed the Wisconsin-Illinois border roughly thirty minutes ago," the other man said. "State Patrol caught his license and tried to pull him over, but so far he's leading them on a high-speed chase."

Gabby gasped at the news. "Why would he do that?" she asked. "He has to know they'll catch him eventually."

"No clue, unless he's feeling desperate," Nate said grimly. "He may figure he has nothing else to lose."

She could barely fathom the idea of the Eric Ambrose she knew giving up. Her former colleague had been cold and calculating, deliberate in his attempts to discredit her.

Although everyone had a breaking point. With the pending litigation and subsequent leave of absence, it was possible Eric was feeling desperate.

"Where is he now?" Shane asked.

"Not sure. They were heading north on Interstate 43 last I heard. Where are you?"

"We're about ten miles from the motel," he answered. "But I think we'll head over to the interstate."

"Don't interfere," Nate warned him. "They'll get him in custody soon, one way or the other."

"Yeah, I know," Shane agreed.

Gabby was very much afraid she knew exactly what that meant. During the course of her career she'd taken care of many trauma patients involved in high-speed crashes. The worst ones were drivers who had drugs or alcohol on board.

Was Eric impaired in some way? Was that

contributing to his irrational behavior? Nothing else made sense.

"Head back toward the motel," Nate urged. "There's nothing you can do until they've arrested him."

"Okay, keep me posted," Shane said.

Gabby disconnected from the call and then reached out to put her hand on his arm. "Can't we head over in that direction?" she asked. "What if Eric hits some innocent bystander? At least I can help provide medical care."

Shane hesitated and she could tell he wanted to head toward the interstate, too. But then he shook his head. "I can't risk your safety, Gabby. I'm sure there are fire trucks trailing the State Police for just that reason."

Gabby sat back in her seat with a frustrated sigh. She really, really wanted to come face-to-face with Eric, to confront him with everything that had happened. Now that they knew he was here in the area for sure, it seemed likely that he was responsible for the kidnapping, breaking into her house, the assault on Richard, and for attacking Royce in her old call room.

She thought about the notes she had locked away in her bank's safe-deposit box. Notes that she'd all but forgotten about until this nightmare started.

The sound of a chopper flying overhead interrupted her thoughts. Peering through the window, she frowned when she realized it wasn't the distinctive blue-and-orange LifeLine helicopter.

"It's a police chopper," Shane said as it passed them by. "That doesn't sound good, Ambrose must still be on the move."

Gabby's stomach clenched and she closed her eyes to pray for the safety of the officers, the innocent people on the road and even for Eric Ambrose.

Dear Lord, please keep everyone safe in Your care.

The tension eased and she glanced over at Shane. "We can't just go back to our motel."

"I know, I feel the same way. I'll head west but will stay on the highways, avoiding the interstate."

Gabby nodded in relief, because even though she couldn't help feeling her skills might be needed if someone got hurt, she didn't want to interfere in the police chase. And she took comfort in the fact that if Eric was indeed responsible for the danger surrounding her, then it would soon be over.

Which meant she wouldn't need to be stuck to Shane like a burr.

Her stomach twisted again and she tried to focus on the police helicopter hovering overhead.

"Shane? Does the interstate go over this highway?"

Before he could respond, she saw a low-slung

black sports car come racing over the bridge ahead, several police cars with their swirling lights and screeching sirens close behind.

There was a large truck hugging the left side of the road, trying to get out of the way, but not far enough. The front bumper of the black sports car clipped the van and spun wildly, with tires squealing.

As if the watching an action movie in slow motion, she saw the sports car flip over the guard-rail and land on its roof on the highway below.

"Pull over, pull over!" Gabby cried, fumbling for the door handle. She could hardly believe what she was seeing, her worst fears coming true.

"Wait for me," Shane ordered, jerking the car off onto the shoulder and stopping abruptly.

Gabby already had her door open and was running toward the upside-down car, her heart in her throat. No matter how she felt about Eric on a personal level, she couldn't deny him the medical assistance he deserved.

She could feel Shane beside her when she reached the car. Dropping down, she peered through the broken driver's-side window, half afraid of what she'd find.

The driver was belted in, hanging upside down. Shane pulled out a knife to cut through the seat belt. Between the two of them, they tugged the driver to safety.

But it wasn't Eric Ambrose. The driver of Eric's car was Joe Chasco.

A shiver crept down Gabby's spine as she reached out to check Joe's pulse. When it was absent, she quickly began CPR. She had no idea why Joe was driving Eric's car, but she was disturbed to know that Eric was still out there. Somewhere.

Maybe even watching them.

THIRTEEN

Shane knelt beside Gabby, intending to help her do CPR, but before he could take his turn at performing chest compressions, the paramedic team arrived.

Three firefighters gently but firmly eased Gabby out of the way, reassuring her that they could take it from here.

"I'm a trauma surgeon at Trinity Medical Center," she protested. But the firefighters didn't budge, obviously too intent on their patient.

Shane took her arm, drawing her off to the side. "They know what they're doing, Gabby. And as talented as you are, even you can't do surgery out here."

"I know, I know," she muttered, pushing her hair away from her face. She turned to face him, her expression serious. "Shane, that's not Eric Ambrose. It's Joe Chasco."

"What?" Since he'd only seen grainy driver's license photos, he hadn't noticed the difference.

But now every one of his instincts went on red alert. He quickly put his arm around Gabby's slender frame, sweeping his gaze over the area that was fast filling up with police and other emergency vehicles. "We need to get out of here. And I'm calling Nate to fill him in on what's going on."

She nodded, clinging to his side and walking along as if she was on pins and needles about what this switcheroo meant. Shane kept his arm around her as they headed back to the sedan. He started the car and then backed away from the emergency vehicles that had partly blocked them in.

"Here," Gabby said, holding out the phone with Nate's name on the screen. "It's on speaker."

He was continuously impressed with her ability to remain calm in a crisis, and it occurred to him that while she clearly wasn't a cop, she often thought like one. She was a great partner.

In more ways than one.

"Yeah?" Nate answered, pulling Shane's attention away from his distracting thoughts.

"Ambrose wasn't the driver, Chasco was," he said bluntly. "They must have swapped cars. We need to get an APB out on Chasco's vehicle."

"Will do," Nate responded. "You'd better make sure to keep the doc safely out of sight."

Yeah, no kidding. "I will. But we have to

figure out what Ambrose's plan is. And why on earth Chasco would go along to this extent."

"Doesn't make sense," Nate muttered. "Unless Ambrose convinced Chasco that he had as much to lose if Gabby's notes were published in a public forum as Ambrose did."

"Maybe, but it still seems extreme. Chasco's in rough shape," Shane told him. "Gabby had to start CPR. There's a really good chance he won't make it."

"Joe's always been a bit reckless," Gabby interjected. "When you mentioned Eric was involved in a high-speed chase, I was surprised, because that isn't Eric's style. He's cold and calculating, to the point of being emotionless. Joe's biggest flaw is that he's arrogant, and I suspect he figured he could handle the chase, no problem."

There was a moment of silence and he and Nate digested Gabby's comments. "Where do you think Ambrose is headed?" Shane finally asked. "The hospital?"

"Maybe," Nate responded. "Could be that he decided that hiring muscle wasn't working so well and that he's better off doing the job himself."

Gabby reached out to Shane. "We need to warn the hospital administration," she told him urgently. "Ambrose is a physician, he'll know how to blend in."

"Understood. Nate? I need you to apprise Griff of this latest turn of events. And I think we should beef up the number of deputies patrolling the hospital inside and out on the grounds. Give everyone Chasco's license plates."

"Okay, but Griff is going to want you there, too," Nate said drily.

Shane knew his buddy was right. The fact that today was his normal day off didn't mean squat when it came to situations like this. The SWAT team was always on call. In fact, he liked that part of his job, being a part of the team.

But no way was he leaving Gabby alone. Not with Ambrose on the loose. "I need someone to cover for me," he said. "What about Isaac?"

"I'll try, but I think he's scheduled to work second shift tonight. Jenna was out of town for a couple of days, but she's back. I'll see if I can catch up with her."

Jenna Reed was one of the few females to make the SWAT team, and was known to be one of their best sharpshooters, right behind Caleb O'Malley. "Okay, thanks. Keep me posted."

"Be warned, you may hear from Griff even if I do get Jenna to cover for you," Nate said before disconnecting from the call.

Shane fully expected to hear from his boss, so the warning wasn't necessary.

Gabby glanced at him, her delicate brow puckered in a frown. "Please don't get in trouble on my account," she said softly. "I'll be fine at the motel if you need to go in."

Shane was already shaking his head before she finished speaking. "No way, Gabby. I'm staying with you, end of discussion."

She was quiet for a long moment. "Thank you, Shane. It means a lot to me that you care so much about keeping me safe. But I hate knowing that you might get in trouble because of me. What if Griff fires you?"

He didn't want to think about losing his job— the career that was so important to him—but nothing was more important than keeping Gabby safe.

Nothing.

And if Griff couldn't accept that, well then he didn't want the job after all.

"It will be fine," he said reassuringly. "Griff will understand." He hoped.

Gabby left her hand resting on his arm and he couldn't help smiling as he drove, despite the rather grim circumstances they faced.

Yeah, he was in trouble as far as Gabby was concerned. Deep, deep trouble.

And for some reason, he couldn't drum up the energy to care.

Gabby noticed that Shane made sure to take the long route back to their motel, just in case Armbrose had in fact been watching them. He kept shifting his gaze to the rearview mirror to be certain they weren't followed.

"I doubt he's behind us," she said.

Shane glanced at her in surprise. "What makes you say that?" he asked curiously.

She shrugged. "The more I think about it, the more I believe Eric used Joe as a diversion. Something to keep the police preoccupied so he could be somewhere else."

A hint of a smile tugged at the corner of Shane's mouth. "You're thinking like a cop," he said with obvious approval.

Her cheeks warmed and she hoped he wouldn't notice. "I also think there's a strong possibility that he might have asked Joe to rent a car, rather than truly swapping rides."

Shane's eyebrows levered upward. "I had that same thought," he said slowly. "Which is part of the reason I'm not leaving you at the motel alone."

She didn't say anything more as he finally pulled into the motel parking lot. This time, she knew the routine and hung back so that Shane could go in first, checking out both rooms to make sure they were clear.

"Let's get these phones charged up and activated," he said. "Then you can notify the hospital administrator about the possible threat."

It didn't take long, since she'd already started charging the first phone while they were in the car. She almost forgot it was Sunday when she picked up the disposable phone; those moments she'd spent with Shane in church seemed to have taken place a long time ago. She missed the sense of peace that had washed over her.

"Hospital operator, how may I direct your call?"

"I need you to page the chief medical officer for me," she said. "I'll hold the line."

Gabby tried to think of how to convince the CMO, Andrew Beecher, of the very real threat. She had no doubt that Ambrose had picked a Sunday on purpose, knowing that there was only a skeletal administrative staff on during weekends.

But what did Eric plan to do? Simply look for her? Or was he planning something more sinister? She didn't trust him one bit. After all, this was the same man who'd put patients in harm's way just to discredit her.

"This is Drew Beecher," a deep male voice said.

"Drew, it's Gabriella," she said. "I'm sorry to bother you on a Sunday, but there's a serious situation you need to know about."

"I'm here at the hospital," her boss admitted. "What's wrong?"

Gabby took a deep breath and let it out slowly. "Did you hear about Brandon being attacked?"

"Yes, I'm the one who ultimately approved your leave of absence."

"I'm in danger, and I believe a surgeon by the name of Eric Ambrose is behind the attacks. And the sheriff's department thinks Eric is on his way to Trinity Medical Center."

"What is this guy capable of?" Drew asked.

"Anything," she admitted candidly. "I think he's probably looking for me, but he is capable of hurting innocent people who might get in his way."

"Are you sure?" Drew asked, his tone laced with skepticism.

She couldn't blame him for his attitude; after all, she wouldn't have believed it herself if she hadn't experienced it firsthand. "Yes, I'm absolutely certain he's unpredictable and dangerous. The sheriff's department is planning to send out several deputies, but you need to help make sure every provider and staff member there is also aware." She glanced at Shane, who was listening intently. "I'll ask the deputies to get you a photograph of Eric and I'd like you to put it up everywhere you can think of."

"All right," Drew agreed slowly. "If you're that worried, we'll take all the necessary precautions."

"Thank you." She momentarily closed her eyes on a flash of relief. Thankfully, Drew Beecher was a decent guy and had believed her. "I'll give you a number where I can be reached."

Shane frowned but didn't say anything as she rattled off the number of her new disposable phone.

"I'll let you know if we find him," Drew said before ending the call.

She set her phone aside with a small sigh. "I hate that I'm causing so much trouble, for you and everyone at the hospital."

"You're not the one at fault," Shane reminded her.

"I know it's Eric's fault. But I was thinking that it might be best if I destroy my notes."

Ironically, Shane didn't try to talk her out of it. "That is a possible solution, except that we would need to let Ambrose know or he'll keep searching."

She ground her teeth in frustration. "And I can't get at the safe-deposit box until tomorrow morning. I shouldn't have kept them after all this time."

"There's no point in beating yourself up over decisions you made a long time ago," Shane admonished gently. "You could have destroyed his career back when the incidents happened, but you didn't. But that does bring up a good point. Why do you think Ambrose came after you now? Just because of the lawsuit?"

Her head started to ache again, not the same

stabbing with an ice-pick type of pain, but a throbbing that had everything to do with stress. "I guess so."

"How did he know you were still here? I imagine physicians move around a bit."

She lifted her shoulder. "I guess maybe he saw the news report."

"That's it!" Shane burst out. "The airport shooting! You were the trauma surgeon on duty that weekend—I saw you being interviewed on television."

She wrinkled her nose. "Don't remind me. I don't know why they were interested in talking to me…it was the victims and their families that deserved the attention."

But Shane didn't seem to be listening. "That was a little over ten days ago, right? And the incident made national news especially since the airport had to be shut down for over twenty-four hours. That has to be it. Ambrose must have seen the news and realized that you were still a threat."

"Maybe," she acknowledged, although she didn't see why the news report would have caused Eric to come after her. It wouldn't be too hard to figure out where she was working if he really wanted to.

The exhaustion that she'd managed to ignore for the past several hours came rushing back.

"I think I'll rest for a while," she murmured,

even though the very idea of sleep seemed impossible. "Will you come and get me if you hear anything about Eric?"

"Of course," Shane assured her. "And I'll be right here if you need anything."

Gabby didn't doubt it for a second. She remembered how he came barreling into her call room in the early-morning hours when he'd heard her screaming in the throes of a nightmare. Hard to believe that was just twelve hours ago.

So much had transpired since then, she thought as she crossed through the connecting door into her room. No wonder she was feeling so mentally and physically drained.

She crawled into bed fully dressed, just in case they needed to leave in a hurry. When she closed her eyes, it wasn't the more horrifying memories that crowded her mind.

No—the one thing that flashed into her mind's eye was the look of surprise and delight on Shane's face when she'd wrapped her arms around his neck and kissed him.

Shane's embrace had managed to banish the fear she'd experienced at being pinned beneath Damon. So much so that all she could think of was Shane. His strong arms, his woodsy scent. The way his kiss had left her wanting more.

Somehow she must have fallen asleep, because when she abruptly woke up, she was surrounded by darkness.

She sat up, shoving her tangled curls away from her face, looking around the small motel room. She frowned, wondering what had woken her up.

A noise? Throwing aside the covers, she eased out of the bed, taking a moment to slide her feet into her comfy walking shoes. She couldn't hear any sounds from the other side of the connecting door, so she assumed Shane must be sleeping too. He certainly deserved the rest.

Heavy curtains shrouded the window, so she lifted a corner, peering out onto the parking lot.

Then she heard it again, a soft tapping sound.

She froze, her heart pounding in her chest. There was no one at her window, and the tapping sounded tinny, as if someone was rapping against glass rather than the hard, dense wooden door.

Shane's room? She drew open her side of the connecting doors and then gently pushed at the door on Shane's side. It swung open easily and she tiptoed into his room.

There it was again, a soft tapping on the window. Fear gripped her by the throat and she crouched over Shane's prone figure to shake his shoulder.

He bolted upright, and she reared back just in time to avoid getting smacked in the face. "Someone's outside," she whispered.

"Hide in the bathroom," Shane commanded

as he reached for his gun. "Don't come out until I tell you it's clear."

She didn't want to leave but sensed that she would only distract him if she stayed. Shane waited until she'd moved back toward the relative safety of the bathroom before crossing over to plaster himself against the wall.

Gabby peered around the door frame, watching with wide eyes as he moved the curtain a slight fraction of an inch. Then with a sigh of disgust, he reholstered his weapon and reached for the door.

"What are you doing, Nate? Trying to give us a heart attack?"

"I didn't want to wake Gabby," the detective said defensively as he entered the room.

"Yeah, because tapping on the window is so much less frightening," she shot back as she crossed the room to where the men stood. Shane flipped on the small light, illuminating the room.

"Sorry," Nate mumbled, rubbing his eyes wearily. "I've been up since yesterday. Guess I'm not thinking too clearly."

Her brief annoyance quickly faded. "What happened? Did Eric show up at the hospital?"

"Not exactly," Nate said, avoiding her direct gaze. "You'd better sit down. I have some bad news."

Gabby sank onto the edge of the bed, her heart racing.

"What's going on?" Shane demanded.

"Eric Ambrose is dead," Nate said bluntly.

"What? How?" Gabby asked in confusion. "I thought you said you didn't find him at the hospital."

"We didn't find him there," Nate clarified. "But one of your neighbors called the police about a possible prowler. So I headed over."

"To my house?" Gabby was still trying to assimilate the information.

"Yeah, to your place. I found Eric Ambrose's body in your backyard."

"That doesn't make any sense," Shane protested.

"There's more. Ambrose had a can of gasoline and a bucket full of rags next to him. I believe he was planning to set fire to your home, but someone must have seen him there and stopped him." Nate lifted his grim gaze to hers. "He was shot execution-style, just like the men who kidnapped you."

"Creighton," she whispered.

"That's the only explanation," Nate agreed.

Goose bumps rippled along her arms and she shivered.

Shane frowned. "So Ambrose wanted to set fire to Gabby's house, presumably to destroy whatever notes she'd kept. But Creighton saw him there and killed him because he thinks that whatever he was searching for originally might be still hidden inside Gabby's house."

Gabby nodded slowly, unable to refute Shane's logic.

"We let ourselves get sidetracked from the real culprit," Shane said in frustration.

"Well, it's not as if Ambrose wasn't a threat," Nate pointed out. "After all, he was planning to set fire to Gabby's house."

Gabby's gaze locked with Shane's. "So you were right all along. The kidnapping is related to my past." Her stomach churned as the truth settled into her bones.

Nate and Shane exchanged a grave look. "It's the only thing that makes sense, Gabby," Shane said with a sigh.

She shook her head helplessly, wishing there was a different answer. Honestly, she would have preferred this be the work of Eric and Joe rather than someone she didn't know.

She shivered again, knowing the danger wasn't over. Far from it. In fact, they were right back where they'd started.

With nothing tangible to go on.

FOURTEEN

Shane dropped onto the edge of the bed next to Gabby, putting a supportive arm around her waist. "I'll keep you safe," he promised in a low husky tone. He hated seeing the stark devastation in her eyes. If Nate hadn't been there, he might have gathered her close and kissed her.

Probably a good thing Nate *was* there. He couldn't afford that kind of distraction. Not when Gabby was still being threatened.

Her attempt to smile wrenched his heart. "I know," she murmured. "And I appreciate that."

"At least we know for sure that Creighton hasn't found what he's looking for," Nate said logically. "And it must be pretty important if he killed Ambrose to prevent Gabby's house from going up in flames."

"Or he's so callous he doesn't mind eliminating anyone who gets in his way," Shane muttered. "The three dead men who kidnapped Gabby is proof of that. He wants something very badly."

"Yes, but what?" Gabby said in an exasperated tone. "We don't have the slightest clue as to what he's looking for. Right now, we're flying completely blind."

Shane knew she was right. But he also knew that the secrets locked inside Gabby's brain held the key. But how to get past her crippling headaches to find them? He glanced over at Nate. "What if we ask Kristine Martin for help?"

Nate frowned, obviously puzzled. "Why would we need the sheriff's department psychologist? Did I miss something? Neither one of us has killed anyone in the line of duty."

"Not for us," Shane said, understanding his buddy's knee-jerk reaction. None of the deputies, or city cops, for that matter, liked having to talk to the department shrink after a shooting. The members of the SWAT team were sometimes given a little leeway, but not much. Rules were rules and that included a mandatory appointment with the psychologist for anyone who shoots and kills in the line of duty.

"Then who?" Nate asked.

"For Gabby."

"Wait a minute," she protested with a frown. "Don't I get a say in this decision?"

Shane nodded, giving her shoulder a reassuring squeeze. "Of course you do. I can't force you to talk to Kristine. But Gabby, what's the alternative? I think it's clear we need to understand what memories you've repressed. Without that link, we won't know what Creighton is after." He cleared his throat. "And he obviously hasn't found what he's looking for yet, not if he's killed Ambrose just to prevent him from torching your house."

"Hawk's right," Nate agreed, scrubbing his hands over his face again. "But we can't call Kristine until morning."

"It is morning," Shane said drily, looking at his watch. "But you're right, I don't think she'd appreciate being woken up at zero two hundred hours."

Nate didn't so much as crack a smile, his eyes dull with fatigue. "Call her whenever you want. I'm beat. I think it's time to head home to get some sleep."

"Stay here," Shane advised. "There are two beds in my room, and quite frankly, you shouldn't drive when you can barely keep your eyes open."

Nate reluctantly nodded. "Okay. Griff has called off all the extra manpower he sent to the hospital, so everyone else will be using this time to recharge, too."

"Good. That's good." Shane rose to his feet. "Take the bed closest to the bathroom," he said to Nate.

"Thanks." The deputy pushed himself away from the wall, making his way across the room toward the second double bed. "Oh, Shane?"

"Yeah?" He paused, turning to look at Nate.

"My police-issue vehicle is parked on the other side of the lobby." He reached into his pocket, pulled out his keys and tossed them to Shane. "In case you want to move it."

He caught the keys midair. "Thanks. Get some sleep."

Shane followed Gabby through the connecting door to enter her room. "I'm willing talk to your psychologist as soon as possible," she said in a quiet voice. "Just tell me when."

"I will." Shane knew Gabby was probably dreading the interview with the department shrink, but she was strong and courageous, willing to do whatever was necessary to find Creighton. "Try not to worry about that now. You should relax and get some rest."

She grimaced and shook her head. "Not likely."

"Do you want to talk?" he asked, sensing Gabby didn't want to be alone.

She hesitated and then shook her head. "No need for both of us to lose sleep."

Shane couldn't make himself leave her alone, so when she sat down on the edge of her bed, he pulled out the desk chair to sit across from her. "I'm not that tired. I'll stay, at least for a while."

This time Gabby's fleeting smile was real. "Thanks, Shane."

"No problem," he said gruffly. "I'm sure Nate's snoring by now, anyway."

She smiled again, brighter this time, and he was glad she was able to find a little humor in their otherwise grim situation. But then her brief smile faded. "It's so frustrating. I wish I could be more help to your investigation."

"What about memories that don't cause a headache?" he asked. "Surely there are some happy ones."

Gabby scooted back so that she was propped comfortably against the headboard. "Yes, but those memories won't likely be of any help to us," she murmured. "I wish my mother was still alive. Then we could simply ask her what happened."

Shane lifted his eyebrows. "Do you think it's strange your mother didn't confide in you?"

Gabby shrugged. "Yes, a little. Especially once she knew that she was dying."

"And you're sure she didn't give you any hints?" he pressed.

Gabby let out a pent-up sigh and spread her hands wide. "Not that I can recall. Toward the end, she was pretty confused...at times she called my stepfather Travis, thinking he was my father."

He grimaced. "I bet that didn't go over well."

"No, it didn't," she said. "But that didn't happen too often. There were other times my mother mumbled words and phrases that didn't make sense."

Shane leaned forward, resting his elbows on his knees. "Like what?"

Gabby looked thoughtful for a moment. "She muttered a lot about the circus and drums, repeating those words over and over like they were stuck in a loop rolling through her mind."

"Circus? Drums?" he repeated with a puzzled frown. "What does that mean?"

"I don't know for sure," she confessed. "The only thing that makes sense is that she was remembering one of the last days we were together as a family."

"Go on," Shane said.

"When my father was alive and we were still living in Las Vegas. We all went to the circus together—me, my godfather, Leo Lewis, and my parents. We had an amazing time. It was a special day for me, and I think it was probably a special day for my mother, too." A nostalgic expression filled her green eyes. "That was the day my father bought her the circus charm bracelet and she wore it all the time. Despite the fact that she married Richard so soon after we relocated, I know she loved my father. I know she must have been shocked and devastated when he died."

He noticed Gabby wince a bit and understood that just thinking about her father caused her headache to return. "Did your mother say anything else?" he asked, trying to divert the subject from anything that might cause her to experience horrible pain.

"Nothing that sticks out as unusual," Gabby whispered. "That was—a very stressful time for me. Made worse by the fact Richard resented my visits."

Shane tried to tamp down a spurt of anger toward her stepfather. Richard Strawn was gone and no matter what he'd done to hurt Gabby in the past, he deserved forgiveness.

Odd how forgiving the people who'd wronged him was easier than forgiving those who had hurt Gabby.

Another indication of how much he cared about her.

"Do you really think your psychologist friend will help?" Gabby asked, interrupting his chaotic thoughts.

"I'm sure she will," he assured her. "Even though I really hate the thought of making you go through that."

She smiled and tucked a curl behind her ear. "I'll be fine. And who knows? Maybe the headaches will go away once the secret is out."

He nodded. "I think that's a distinct possibility. And remember, God will be with you the entire time. He can help you fight through the pain."

Her gaze turned thoughtful. "I hadn't considered that before, but you're right. I think praying could help get me through it."

Shane was thrilled that Gabby was open to believing in God and prayer. Oh, he knew that she had a long way to go—praying with him and attending church once wasn't going to make her a Christian overnight. But she was on the right path.

He wanted to be with her throughout the rest of her journey, too. By her side. Helping her. Supporting her.

Gabby yawned and he knew that she was relaxed enough to sleep. He rose and crossed over toward the connecting door. "Time for you to get some sleep," he told her gently. "Good night, Gabby."

"Good night, Shane."

It took every ounce of willpower he possessed not to kiss her again. He slipped through to his room and made sure the connecting door wasn't open more than a half inch to give her the privacy she needed.

He grinned wryly when he heard Nate's deep breathing from the other bed. After pulling the keys out of his pocket, he considered moving Nate's SUV but then decided against it.

Time to restrategize, and maybe even go to a new location in the morning. But only after setting up a meeting with Kristine to work with Gabby.

Shane drifted off to sleep, convinced that once

they had the information they needed, they'd be able to track down and arrest Creighton.

Before he found Gabby.

Gabby woke up early feeling refreshed despite Nate's late arrival and his disturbing news about Eric Ambrose's death. For a little while she simply enjoyed the tranquil moment, opening her heart and her mind to prayer.

Thank you for this wonderful day, Lord, and help me follow Your chosen path. Amen.

Peace settled over her like a soft, comfortable blanket, making Gabby realize how important it was to believe in God and to have faith in Him. She owed Shane a debt of gratitude for showing her the way. She had no idea how she'd managed to exist before, without having faith or believing in God.

Maybe that was the whole point. That believing in God helped bring true meaning into her life.

Deep thoughts for so early in the morning, she thought with a rueful smile. She crawled out of bed and freshened up in the bathroom. When she finished, she made herself a cup of coffee with the courtesy coffeemaker provided by the motel.

Her stomach rumbled with hunger and she wondered if there might be a continental breakfast available in the lobby. When they'd arrived early yesterday morning, she thought she remembered seeing some food on the counter.

The more she thought about the possibility of breakfast, the more she wanted to walk over to get something to eat. Crossing over to the connecting door, she opened her side and listened for any sound coming from Shane's room.

Total silence.

Knowing the guys deserved to sleep, she grabbed her plastic room key and eased outside.

The crisp autumn air made her shiver and she was surprised to see there was a dense fog hovering over the motel parking lot. So thick she couldn't make out Nate's car, which she knew he'd parked on the other side of the lobby entrance.

Her sweater didn't provide much warmth, so she crossed her arms over her chest and hurried along the sidewalk toward the lobby. She ducked inside, grateful for the warmth.

The lobby was pretty much empty, but thankfully there was a platter of bagels and muffins, along with a large pot of coffee. There was also a mini juice bar. Gabby helped herself to a blueberry muffin and a small glass of orange juice before carrying her breakfast to one of the square tables.

There was a flat-screen television hanging on the wall, and the weatherman was talking about the fog being caused by their proximity to Lake Michigan.

She knew from experience the fog wouldn't hang around for long. Lake Michigan was large, but it wasn't the ocean, so they didn't have the same problems that places like San Francisco had. Gabby took her time eating breakfast, feeling a little guilty when she added a cinnamon and raisin bagel to her plate once she finished the muffin.

The bagel was just as delicious, and she told herself it was better not to let the food go to waste, but just then two semitruck drivers walked in to eat breakfast, too, loudly complaining about how the fog would put them behind schedule.

She listened to them as she finished eating, feeling much better once she had food in her belly. From their conversation she knew they were headed south, toward Chicago, and they weren't happy about the fog being a problem down there, too.

After finishing her breakfast, she debated taking plates of food back for Shane and Nate, but the way the motel clerk was staring intently at her from behind the counter made her uncomfortable. Was he upset that she'd eaten more than her fair share? Ridiculous, the two truck drivers had piled their plates high with baked goods.

She tried to ignore the clerk's glare but decided

against taking anything back for Shane and Nate. The guys could come here to get their own food, and if they didn't hurry, there probably wouldn't be anything left.

"Drive safely," she said when she walked past the truck drivers to toss out her garbage.

"We will. Have a nice day, ma'am," the older of the two replied.

Gabby went back outside, hunching her shoulders against the chilly air. She wasn't particularly thrilled to go back to the stuffy motel room. Maybe Shane would allow her to go for a run. She hadn't been able to exercise since this nightmare started.

She quickly shoved the wave of self-pity aside. What was *wrong* with her? She was lucky to be here at all. And she needed to remember that it was only due to Shane that she was still safe and sound.

As she approached the door to her room, she noticed that the maid's cart was parked adjacent to the entranceway, about a foot from the side of the building. She was surprised the maids were up and about so early, it was barely seven in the morning. And why would the maid be cleaning her room? Her things were still inside and checkout time wasn't until eleven o'clock in the morning.

Although it could be that the maid was cleaning

the truck drivers' rooms. Maybe they'd checked out, despite the fog.

She was about to pull out her key when a warning tingle lifted the hairs on the back of her neck. She hesitated a second too late. Before she could move, a man's arm grabbed her from behind, wrapping tightly around her throat, cutting off her supply of oxygen. Then he pressed the cold tip of a gun firmly against her temple.

She froze, struggling to breathe.

"You've caused me a lot of trouble, Gabriella," the man hissed in her ear. "But it's over. You're going to give me what I want, what's rightfully mine, aren't you?"

Gabby tried to nod, but the viselike grip around her neck prevented her from moving. She considered kicking him in the kneecap or stomping on his instep, but what if the gun went off?

No, she couldn't risk it. Better to go with him now, and look for a chance to escape later.

"Come on," he muttered harshly, easily dragging her backward as if she didn't weigh more than a feather. His movement tightened his arm around her throat and tiny red dots danced in front of her eyes as she struggled to breathe around the thick muscles of his biceps and forearm.

The fog surrounded them, making her feel as if she was completely alone with the gunman.

With Creighton.

How had he found her here at the motel? And especially her room number? Obviously he must have been hiding near the maid's cart. Had he bribed the motel clerk? Was that why the guy had been staring at her so intently?

She wanted to scream for Shane and Nate, wishing one of them would wake up and realize she was gone. But she could barely breathe, let alone scream. Every step Creighton took drew her farther away from the safety of the motel.

Soon she couldn't even see the building.

Fear was bitter on her tongue as she tried to think of a plan to escape. She was smart, surely she could outthink a thug like Creighton?

But she didn't have a scalpel in her pocket this time. Nothing but a plastic motel key. And unfortunately she knew Shane wasn't in a position where he could run after her, coming to her rescue in the nick of time by hitching a ride on the back of a pickup truck.

Maybe once they reached their destination she'd be in a better position to get away from the gunman. Creighton would have to loosen his grip on her sometime. She couldn't give him what he wanted if she couldn't talk or breathe.

Yet she knew with a sick sense of certainty that once Creighton got what he wanted, he wouldn't need her anymore.

Once she'd served her purpose, he'd likely kill

FIFTEEN

Shane woke up, instantly alert, his instincts screaming at him that something was wrong.

He rolled out of bed, barely glancing at Nate's slumbering form. Thankfully he'd slept in his clothes, so he shoved his feet into his shoes and grabbed his gun as he strode toward the connecting doors.

Rapping sharply against the wood, he only waited a second or two before pushing her side of the door open. "Gabby?"

A chill snaked down his back when he saw the room was empty. The bathroom door was open, but he crossed over to check inside anyway. She wasn't in there, either.

Where in the world was she?

He noticed several details seemingly at once. The coffeemaker had been used, her duffel bag was still sitting on the floor beside her bed and her shoes were missing.

Rushing toward the door, he yanked it open,

peering out into the foggy mist. The maid's cart was sitting to the right side of Gabby's door, but there was no sign of cleaning personnel.

Or of Gabby.

Muttering under his breath, he raced back into his room to rouse Nate. He bent down and shook the other man's shoulder. "Get up, Gabby's missing. We need to search for her."

"What?" Nate rolled over, blinking the sleep from his eyes. It didn't take long for the news to sink in, and his buddy quickly shot out of bed. "Don't panic, it's possible she went to the lobby to get something to eat."

"I'll check there, you sweep the grounds," Shane ordered.

Nate nodded as he shoved his feet into his shoes. They quickly split up, heading in opposite directions.

Shane found the lobby was empty and there were a few stray bagels sitting on a platter next to a coffeepot and a juice bar. He strode over to the guy behind the counter who was eyeing him warily. "Have you seen a woman in here this morning?" he demanded. "A slender woman with red-gold curly hair?"

The guy's eyes shifted right and then left, beads of sweat popping out on his pale half-balding forehead. "Um, yeah. I saw her. She was here, eating breakfast."

Shane's instincts went into overdrive and he

grabbed the guy by the front of his shirt, yanking him forward. "What did you do?" he demanded in a stern tone. "Did someone ask about her? Did you tell someone where she was?"

"Lemme go," the clerk whined. "I didn't do nuthin!"

"Where is she?" Shane growled, not believing his innocence for a second. He tightened his grip on the guy's shirt, hanging on to his temper with considerable effort. "Who paid you?"

"Some guy came in earlier this morning, asking to see the pretty redhead. Mentioned something about being her long-lost uncle and traveling quite a distance to see her, that's all." The clerk looked scared to death, but Shane wasn't about to let him off the hook that easily.

"When did he get here? What did he look like? What was he driving?" The questions were rapid-fire and the guy cowered, ducking his head.

"Came in early, right at the start of my shift. He's tall and brawny and has short blond hair. I don't know what the dude's driving."

Shane nodded tersely. "Now tell me *exactly* what he said to you."

"He gave me some sob story about being away from his family for a really long time and told me he wanted to surprise his niece. I said it was against the rules, but he slipped me a fifty so I let him know what room she was in. Afterward, I was surprised to see her here alone, eating breakfast. No uncle in sight. She left twenty minutes ago. That's all, man, that's all. I promise I didn't do anything!"

Shane let go of his shirt, fighting a wave of anger. "You took fifty bucks from a killer and you better hope I find her before it's too late, or I'll be back to arrest you for being his accomplice."

The clerk paled and patted his pockets. "I'll give you the money back! It's no big deal! You can have it back!"

Shane ignored him, jogging outside to find Nate, his heart pounding in his chest and his throat thick with fear.

Creighton had Gabby.

And a twenty-minute lead. Maybe less, depending on how long it took him to grab her. But not much less.

"Nate, where are you?" he shouted as he tried to peer through the fog.

"Back here. I found the maid."

Shane followed the sound of Nate's voice to the small alcove at the end of the row of rooms, near the stairway leading to the second floor. There was a vending machine tucked in the corner and Nate was kneeling beside a young woman slouched against it, her eyes closed and her skin pale.

"Is she alive?" Shane asked as he joined them.

"Yeah, she has a pulse," Nate confirmed. "I

think he just knocked her unconscious. I've called 911, there's an ambulance on the way."

Shane glanced helplessly around the area. "I'll get the desk clerk to sit here with her. We have to go. Creighton has Gabby."

"What?" Nate demanded.

"The clerk ratted her out for fifty bucks. We need to go find her!"

"Go where?" Nate asked logically. "We don't know where he's taking her."

"Then we have to figure it out!" Shane wanted to rant and rave at the top of his lungs, panic and fear threatening to overwhelm him. "We have to be smarter than he is. Don't you get it? Once he has what he needs, there's no reason to keep Gabby alive."

Nate nodded slowly. "I know, I hear you. Okay, so where do you think he'd take her?"

Shane raked his hands through his hair, wishing he had a good answer. "Maybe to her house. He prevented Ambrose from torching the place, so it could be that he believes what he wanted is still there."

"All right, we'll head there first," Nate agreed. "I don't hear the ambulance yet, so we'll need the desk clerk to come out here to stay with the maid."

"Gladly." Shane ran back to the lobby, pinning the guy behind the counter with a hard gaze. "I need you outside, now."

The guy cringed, hanging back. "No, leave me alone!"

"That guy who gave you the fifty so he could grab the redhead also knocked your maid unconscious," Shane explained in a terse tone. Every second he wasted here seemed like a lifetime. "I need you to come outside and stay with her until the ambulance arrives. Understand?"

The guy blanched but then nodded. "All right," he agreed, the seriousness of the situation finally getting through to him.

Shane led the way back to where Nate had remained with the injured maid. The desk clerk looked shocked to see her propped against the vending machine.

"I didn't know," he whispered. "I'm sorry, Carla, I didn't know!"

Shane let go of his anger on a heavy breath, knowing that the clerk really hadn't realized the consequences of his actions.

"Let's go," he said to Nate as his buddy rose to his feet.

"I'm with you."

Shane ran back inside the motel room to get the keys. Seconds later, he and Nate were inside the police-issue vehicle. Nate took the wheel, leaving Shane feeling restless and anxious, needing to do something.

Anything.

"Better call for backup," Nate advised, sending Shane a sidelong glance. "Griff needs to know about this turn of events."

Shane nodded, knowing Nate was right. He reached for the radio, wishing he was wearing his SWAT gear. Not that he was going to let that stop him from going in to rescue Gabby.

"Dispatch, this is unit twelve requesting to speak with Lieutenant Vaughn."

"Ten-four, unit twelve, hold the line."

Shane waited impatiently for Griff to answer. "What's going on, Hawk?"

"Dr. Fielding was taken from the motel," Shane said bluntly. "I'm here with Nate... We believe Creighton has her."

"What's your twenty?" Griff asked.

"Heading east on the interstate but slow moving because of the fog. We're checking out Dr. Fielding's residence first."

"Negative," Griff snapped. "The area remains cordoned off as an active crime scene, and the techs are heading out there as soon as the fog lifts. I highly doubt Creighton will risk going there."

Shane ground his teeth together in frustration, knowing that his boss was right. "Okay, then we'll check out her stepfather's place. I'm requesting backup—no lights and sirens—along with extra SWAT gear for me."

There was a pause before Griff responded. "Ten-four. I'll send two squads to meet you. Do you have a second destination in mind if she's not there?"

Unfortunately, he didn't. There was no reason for Creighton to take her to the hospital; after all, the place would be swarming with personnel, even at this early hour in the morning. And it wasn't likely that Gabby would store personal, private information there anyway.

So where would Creighton go? Especially if her house was an active crime scene?

His heart sank to the bottom of his gut. Anywhere. Creighton could take Gabby just about anywhere. And he couldn't bear to think that Creighton may attempt to torture the information out of her.

"I don't know," he admitted in a choked voice. "We'll consider the possibilities once we verify she's not being held at Strawn's house."

"Ten-four," Griff agreed. "Stay in touch."

Shane disconnected from the radio, every muscle in his body tense to the point he felt as if he might shatter.

He didn't want to consider the possibility they may not find Gabby at Richard's house, but forced himself to think through other options.

If Creighton was connected to her father's death twenty-one years ago in Las Vegas, where could they be now? At a local casino? Not likely, the casinos here weren't the same kind as in Vegas.

And all of this had to be connected to Gabby's father's death. So where else could she be?

An abandoned warehouse? Isolated cabin in the woods? Maybe they needed to go back to the clearing off Highway 60? Did Creighton have a place out there?

"I'm sorry," Nate said, breaking the strained silence.

Shane shook his head. "It's not your fault Gabby was taken from the motel. Creighton paid the desk clerk fifty bucks to tell him what room Gabby was in."

"But the only way Creighton could have possibly found the motel in the first place is because of me," Nate said grimly. "He must have followed me last night. I didn't think anyone was behind me, but somehow I must have missed him."

Shane glanced at his friend, remembering how exhausted Nate had been when he arrived at the motel. Was it possible he missed a tail? Somehow, Shane doubted it.

"It's not your fault, Nate. If anyone is to blame, it's me. I thought about relocating last night, but I figured we should wait until morning."

"Oh, man!" Nate abruptly pulled off the highway, bumping over the shoulder as he sharply braked. "What if he has a tracking device on the car?"

Shane was torn with indecision. Every instinct he possessed made him want to race to Richard's house, to be sure Gabby wasn't being held there. But if Nate was right, and he hadn't missed a tail, then the tracking device was still on the vehicle.

And they'd only be announcing their arrival. Creighton could take Gabby and leave again, before they caught him.

"You're right, we need to make sure. Do you have an extra flashlight?" Shane asked, rummaging through the glove box.

"Here," Nate replied, pulling up the cover over the center console. He handed Shane the flashlight, taking the other off his uniform utility belt.

"I'll take the front, you take the back." Shane slid out of the car and then turned over to scoot under the vehicle on his back, using the flashlight to scan the undercarriage.

He forced himself to go slow so he wouldn't miss anything, no easy feat when he desperately wanted to get back on the road.

After what seemed like hours, but was only ten minutes, he saw the tiny tracking device. "I found it," he breathed.

Dislodging the device didn't take long, and when he had it in his hand, he inched back out from beneath the car.

He showed it briefly to Nate, who stared at it in grim silence. "Not your fault," Shane reassured him, before throwing the device as far into the field as possible.

Nate didn't say anything as he climbed back

into the driver's seat. Shane knew his buddy was still kicking himself, but at this point, all they could do was to move forward from here.

He closed his eyes and prayed for Gabby's safety as Nate started the car up and merged back onto the freeway.

He hoped and prayed they would find Gabby at Richard's house. Because if they didn't, the odds of them finding her alive dropped significantly.

And he couldn't bear the idea of losing Gabby.

Gabby stared helplessly down at the metal handcuffs Creighton had slapped on her wrists one-handed, holding his gun steady with the other. She hadn't dared try to escape the moving vehicle, convinced that he wouldn't hesitate to shoot her in the leg to slow her down.

No, at this point she wasn't going to win a physical fight against him. Creighton was younger than she'd thought, only mid-to-late forties by her estimation, with blond hair and narrow icy gray eyes. He looked as if he lifted weights on a regular basis—his arms were as thick as tree trunks. She imagined he'd left bruises around her neck from when he'd grabbed her.

She knew only too well that he'd kept her alive because she had something he wanted.

Knowledge was power, at least for the moment.

Creighton muttered a vile curse beneath his

breath when he saw that there were police vehicles parked outside her home. She wanted to smile at the fact that his heinous crimes were now working against him.

She didn't bother to point out that he shouldn't have left Ambrose in her backyard. No sense in angering a cold-blooded killer.

What she needed was a way to outsmart him. But how?

"I know what you want," she whispered.

He abruptly turned to glare at her. "You do? Then tell me where you have them?"

Them? Her first clue wasn't very helpful. He was looking for more than one thing. Papers? Was that why he'd focused his search on her office and Richard's office?

"In a safe place," she hedged. "Where no one will find them."

"You'll take me to them, or I'll start shooting you in places that will make you scream in pain but won't kill you."

The evil glint in his eye sent chills down her spine, but she kept ahold of herself. His goal was obviously to scare her, and she refused to allow him the satisfaction of knowing how close he was to succeeding.

"You don't want me to have to hurt you, do you?" he sneered.

"N-no." For a moment a horrible memory

flashed in her mind, an image of being in her father's study, listening to him pleading for his life.

But then the image was gone, vanishing on a wave of pain so terrible it twisted her stomach and stole her breath.

No! She needed to remember!

"Where are they?" Creighton demanded harshly.

She fought against the pain, keeping her voice even with an effort. "They're hidden at Richard's house," she finally admitted, hoping, praying that Shane and Nate had figured out by now that she was gone. That they'd manage to find her at Richard's house.

Before it was too late.

"I knew it," Creighton said, slamming his fist on the steering wheel of the car. "The old man caught me searching his office so I knocked him out, but then the cops arrived before I could finish searching the place."

"Didn't you go back?" she asked.

"Not right away, but I did go to see your dear old stepfather in the hospital," Creighton said in a snide tone. "Did you know that? I tried to get him to talk, but he wouldn't cooperate."

Gabby caught her breath. "You killed him," she whispered.

Creighton let out an evil laugh that made her shiver. "Yeah, because I needed to make sure he wouldn't wake up later and give me away. Anyone can push a syringe full of air into his veins and it was easy to slip away before any-one saw me."

Grief and despair welled up inside her. Rich-ard had died of an air embolus not from a blood clot. Her stepfather had been another of Creigh-ton's casualties.

Just like she would be, if she didn't figure out what paperwork he was looking for.

"How did you find me after all these years?" she asked in a feeble attempt to keep him talk-ing. Thankfully, the fog made driving tricky and Creighton couldn't go as fast as he likely wanted to.

Although, that meant Shane and Nate had the same disadvantage.

"I got lucky," Creighton said. "Saw you giv-ing a news conference after that airport shoot-ing. Have to say, I was surprised to find you were some hotshot surgeon. I might not have recog-nized you after twenty-one years, but your red hair and facial features were so much like your father's, and having the same last name cinched it."

Gabby's pulse spiked at his words. Creigh-ton had obviously been acquainted with her fa-ther, but knowing he'd seen her, maybe even had watched her, made her feel sick to her stomach.

She should have listened to Jake Walsh, the federal marshall who'd relocated her and her mother after her father's death. She never should have changed her name back to Fielding the minute she turned eighteen. At the time, she'd done that in a rare flash of defiance. As a way to show Richard and her mother that she didn't care if she wasn't a part of their family.

But, in fact, that act of rebellion had led Creighton straight to her all these years later.

For what? What did he want from her?

Money. Of course, this had to be about greed and money.

But she didn't have any money, not in the way he might have assumed a doctor would.

But her father may have had money, she realized with a sinking sensation. Her head throbbed, but she forced herself to ignore the pain. Her father had been an accountant for one of the largest casinos in Vegas. What if Shane and Nate had been right all along?

What if her father, the man she'd idolized growing up, had actually been a criminal? Embezzling money that didn't belong to him?

Money that Creighton would continue to kill for, until he had it for his own.

SIXTEEN

Shane peered through the fog, relieved to note it wasn't as thick as before. The sun was doing its job, burning away the remnants of moisture that clung to the air. "Take this next exit," he directed. "We'll come up on Richard's house from the back way."

Nate didn't argue, hadn't said much at all since Shane had found the GPS device planted beneath the car.

Shane used his radio to update Griff. "This is unit twelve, our ETA to the Strawn residence is less than ten minutes," he said.

"Ten-four," Griff responded. "Unit seven is on scene, looking to get in sharpshooter position. Your extra SWAT gear is in the vehicle."

Shane understood that unit seven was Jenna Reed, and he was glad to have her as backup. Once she had Creighton in the crosshairs, he was confident she'd make the shot to put him out of commission.

"Ten-four," he said, acknowledging the information. "We're not going to get too close, we'd rather go in on foot."

There was only a brief hesitation before Griff answered. "Ten-four."

"You should have told him about the tracking device," Nate said grimly. "He deserves to know what happened."

Shane shrugged. "Doesn't matter now... There's no threat since we got rid of it. Besides, there'll be time for a full confession after we rescue Gabby."

"I hope they're at the house," Nate muttered.

"They *will* be," Shane said, infusing confidence in his tone. "Gabby's smart...she'd find a way to lure him there, knowing it's the most logical place for us to find her."

"I didn't trust her at first," Nate confessed. "I thought you were too emotionally involved, so I was determined to consider every possible option. I obviously went too far the other way."

Shane sighed. "You were right, I was—and still am—too emotionally involved with her. But we're going to find Gabby, Nate. I've been praying a lot and I believe God is with us, guiding us."

"I hope you're right." There was still a hint of doubt lacing Nate's tone.

"I am. Pull over in that parking lot," he said, indicating the strip mall that was located to the left. "Strawn's place is roughly four blocks behind those buildings, right in the middle of a high-end subdivision."

"Lots of people around, heading to work this time of the morning," Nate observed as he parked at the end of the parking lot. "Do you think he'll risk it?"

"Yeah, I do," Shane said, hoping he was right. He desperately needed to believe Gabby and Creighton were there because the alternative was too painful to contemplate. "Let's move."

He and Nate slid out of the car and Shane led the way through several neighbors' yards, glad that his buddy was still wearing his uniform, his badge clearly displayed on his chest. It was broad daylight, not exactly the easiest time to sneak up on someone. Still, he wondered how many home owners might come outside to gape, giving them away?

Hopefully, most people would be at work.

When they crossed the street of the third block, Shane slowed down, signaling Nate to take cover. He spotted Jenna's vehicle parked alongside the road and crossed over to pull out the SWAT gear she'd left in the backseat. Rather than wasting time changing into a full uniform, he pulled on the bullet-resistant vest over his sweater and grabbed extra ammunition, just in case he needed it.

When he finished, he continued on his path

between houses. This particular neighborhood had many big, fancy homes with large yards and an abundance of trees, a fact that worked in their favor. He and Nate took turns moving through the backyard that butted up against Richard's property, using bushes and trees for coverage.

Shane swept his gaze across the area, searching for any sign of Gabby or Creighton. When he saw a tan sedan parked in the driveway, his lungs filled with a wave of satisfaction. He knew full well that Richard's car, a vintage Corvette, had been parked in the garage the last time he'd been here. Which meant the sedan had to belong to Creighton.

Gabby was here!

He crouched between a large fire bush and turned back to look at Nate, who was standing beside a large maple tree. Shane gestured to the sedan and then put his thumb up, as an indication they were on the right track.

His partner nodded and pointed upward. Shane's gaze traveled up to the lowest branches of the tree. Jenna Reed was perched there, holding her M40 Sniper Rifle ready, the business end pointed directly at the house. She didn't notice him and Nate standing there, since she was peering intently through the scope.

Could she see Gabby and Creighton inside? There were dozens of windows on the house and he had to think for a minute to orient himself, remembering the interior layout from the last time he'd been there.

Richard's study was located on this side of the house in the corner facing west and south. Gabby was smart—even though Creighton had searched the study, she'd find a way to convince him that he'd missed what he was looking for.

At least, that's what he hoped she'd do.

Now that he knew that his backup was in place, along with the possibility of a second sniper—hopefully, Caleb O'Malley, on the opposite side of the house—Shane decided it was time to make their move.

Once again, he took the lead, keeping low as he made his way across the yard to the side of the house. Inching along the side, he crept up to the front door. Testing the knob, he was relieved to find it unlocked.

Mistake number one for Creighton. Or maybe it was mistake number two, since coming to Richard's in the first place could be considered a grievous error.

Shane eased stealthily into Richard's house, practically hugging the wall to avoid any chance of stepping on a squeaky floorboard and alerting Creighton to his presence.

Once he cleared the foyer, he could hear voices coming from inside the study. Two voices, male and female.

Relief that Gabby was still alive filled his chest, infusing him with fierce conviction.

Gabby would not suffer at Creighton's hands for much longer. He'd do whatever was necessary to get her safe.

Sacrificing his life for hers, if necessary.

Gabby held her cuffed wrists awkwardly in front of her as she watched Creighton warily. He still had his gun trained on her, but he was standing behind Richard's desk, looking at her intently.

"Well? Now what?" he asked impatiently.

She wasn't sure how much longer she could hold him off. Creighton had grown irritated with her questions, and she'd already taken him through the right side of Richard's desk only to come up empty-handed.

All too soon, he'd realize she'd been lying to him about where the papers were.

And she was very much afraid that he'd shoot her in the kneecap, the way he'd threatened to, in order to make her scream with pain yet live to tell him what she knew.

"I know I've seen the file," she repeated for what seemed like the tenth time. "It has to be in one of his desk drawers. I asked him to hide it amongst his business paperwork, in a place no one would look for it."

Creighton's gaze narrowed suspiciously. "Don't

lie to me," he threatened in a low, dangerous tone. "Or I'll make sure you regret it."

She swallowed hard and wondered if it was time to change tactics. She'd been praying steadily from the moment Creighton had kidnapped her from the motel. And though she knew it was important not to lose faith, it sure wasn't easy.

Please, Lord, please give me strength and courage!

Creighton bent down to go through the last desk drawer and she knew she couldn't delay a minute longer.

"Okay, okay, you're right," she said abruptly. "I didn't give Richard the information because I memorized it. Everything you need to know is in my memory."

Creighton's head snapped up to hers, his face turning an ugly shade of red and his eyes cold with fury. He slowly straightened and then deliberately tipped the point of his gun down, toward her legs. At this close range he couldn't possibly miss.

She took a hasty step back, raising her cuffed wrists in a gesture of surrender. "Wait! Don't shoot! You don't understand—I have an eidetic memory. A photographic memory! I can remember every single detail, can re-create what you're looking for right here, right now..." she said in a rush.

He stared at her for a long moment, as if he didn't believe her. But then he threw his head back and laughed. "A photographic memory, just like your father, eh? It took a while to figure out that he used his ability to memorize things to skim money away from the casinos and into his overseas bank accounts so easily. He got away with it, too, until my uncle and the owner of the casino, Frankie Palmetto, got suspicious and hired someone else to double-check your father's work."

For a moment she winced, the pain returning as she realized her father had been guilty of a pretty significant crime. Why had he used his incredible talent to steal? Why hadn't he just taken her and her mother away, somewhere safe, instead of risking his life for money?

Knowing she'd inherited his memory made her feel sick.

But then she realized that Creighton had given her exactly what she needed. Bank accounts! Of course, that's what he was looking for. Overseas bank accounts that still held the money her father had embezzled all those years ago.

Abruptly, the memory she'd repressed as a child came rushing back to her.

Her father had been working from home that day, and she'd been sitting on the floor in his study, next to the windows beneath the golden rays of sunlight. He hadn't minded her being there, as long as she was quiet, so she buried her nose in her favorite book, The Black Stallion. *When the doorbell rang, her father got up to answer it, there was a loud noise, the front door banging open.*

Her father had looked shocked and then scared.

"Hide, Gabriella! Under the desk. Don't come out and don't make a sound. No matter what happens, don't let them see you!"

Gabby had taken her book and crawled under the desk, curling into a ball as small as possible. Her father shoved the desk chair in front of her to help keep her hidden from view.

At first, the men had only talked to her father, demanding the account numbers. Her father denied having them, but then she heard a harsh slap and knew that someone had been hit. There was another slap, and then another, and when she heard her father cry out in pain, she covered her ears and closed her eyes, wishing desperately that her father would just give them the account numbers so the bad men would go away and leave them alone.

Then there was a long silence, before one of the men accused the other of going too far.

"You hit him too hard! He's dead, you idiot! You've killed him! Now we'll never get the account numbers!"

There was another loud thud, and from

beneath the wheels of the rolling chair, she saw her father's bruised and battered face pressed against the carpet, blood seeping into the beige fibers, spreading into a dark red stain.

Her father was dead.

She thought she might have screamed, but the men didn't find her, so she must have only screamed in her mind. Over and over again...

"Are you sure?" Creighton demanded, drawing Gabby back to the present. "Are you sure you have them memorized?"

For a moment she stood there, looking at him uncertainly. Then she gathered every ounce of her strength together, knowing that she had to hang on long enough for Shane to find her.

"Yes," she said, injecting confidence into her voice. "I have all the bank account numbers memorized. If you give me a few minutes, I'll write them down for you."

Creighton reached out and roughly grabbed her arm, yanking her around the desk. He pushed her into the chair and handed her a pen and a pad of paper. Holding the pen was awkward with the handcuff's on but not impossible.

"Get writing," he commanded, pushing the tip of the gun against her temple as if to remind her he was armed and dangerous. "And don't think of trying to fool me—I have a computer and we're not going anywhere until I've checked them out."

When he pulled a tablet out of the inside of his coat pocket, her heart sank. This was it. The minute he checked the bank account numbers, he'd know she was lying.

Gabby glanced around the room, searching for a way out. She must not have stalled long enough, because she thought for sure Shane would be there by now.

"Well? Hurry up!" Creighton said, turning on his portable computer.

Her fingers tightened on the pen, and she wondered, briefly, if she could stab him with it, gaining the advantage long enough to escape.

Probably not. He'd no doubt shoot her. Her gaze went to the window, thinking that the bright sunlight was just as it had been back on the day her father had died. There was a flash of bright light in the tree that made her frown, but an instant later it was gone.

Had she imagined it? Maybe.

"You were there that day, in my father's study, weren't you?" she asked, risking a glance at Creighton. "You must have been young then, in your early twenties."

For the first time since this nightmare started, Creighton looked surprised. "How did you know?"

"I was there that day, hiding under my father's desk," she said. "You didn't realize that I was there, listening as you tried to beat the account numbers out of him with your fists. You killed him, didn't you? You hit him too hard and killed him without getting the account numbers you wanted."

Creighton gaped at her, clearly stunned by the news. She saw the barest hint of a shadow near the doorway, and her heart raced with anticipation.

Was Shane there? Waiting to make his move?

"You didn't realize I'd witnessed my father's murder, did you?" Gabby hoped that by talking she'd distract Creighton from noticing Shane. "You hadn't anticipated that me and my mother would be whisked away into witness protection as a result."

Creighton's face got red again and she forced a harsh laugh from her tight throat.

"Everything backfired on you that day. If you hadn't killed my father, you would have had the account numbers and would have gotten away free and clear."

"Shut up," he growled. "Shut up or I'll shoot you right now."

"No, you won't. Not until I give you the account numbers," she said, egging him on.

She saw the flash in the trees and decided Shane must have backup stationed outside. But they wouldn't take a shot at Creighton as long as he had his gun on her. Now was the time to make her move. As soon as she was out of the way, they'd have a clear shot at Creighton.

Shoving back the chair, she slid down to the floor and dived beneath the desk.

The minute she hit the floor, the sound of gunfire and glass shattering echoed through the room. Gabby was tempted to cover her ears, just the way she had as a child, but she resisted, knowing she needed to listen.

Another gunshot made her cringe with fear. Shane? Had Creighton taken a shot at him? What if Shane was hit?

She poked her head out from beneath the desk, her heart lodging in her throat when she couldn't see Shane.

But then she heard his voice. "Creighton's down! He's been shot twice, I need a paramedic team."

Creighton was injured. Shane wasn't hurt. It was over.

Her nightmare was finally over.

She awkwardly staggered to her feet. Shane was kneeling beside Creighton's prone figure, holding pressure on his abdomen where she presumed Creighton had been shot.

Her trauma surgeon instincts kicked in. Despite everything Creighton had done, to her father and to all the people he'd killed since then, she knew she had to help.

"Can you get these cuffs off?" she asked, coming over to crouch beside Shane. "I need to be able to use my hands."

He glanced at her, relief evident as he raked his gaze over her, as if reassuring himself that she wasn't harmed. "Hey, Nate! We need handcuff keys in here, now!"

Nate materialized from the other room, crossing over to her. Gabby held her wrists out so he could use the key to unlock the cuffs.

"Are you sure you're all right?" Shane asked in a gruff tone. "He didn't hurt you?"

"I'm fine," she murmured, glad when the cuffs dropped away from her skin. She hoped they wouldn't notice the bruises around her throat. There wasn't time to worry about them now. "Where is he hit?"

"He has an abdominal wound and a right-shoulder wound," Shane said grimly.

"Keep pressure on his abdomen while I check out the chest wound," she said, going around to kneel on the other side of Creighton's body, facing Shane. "Nate, I need towels, lots of towels."

"On it," Nate said, jumping to his feet. She could see the entrance wound in Creighton's shoulder and applied pressure the same way Shane was doing on the abdominal wound.

"Here," Nate said, tossing down several towels.

"Thanks." She folded several towels into thick squares. She pressed the pad over the entry wound in his shoulder and then leaned over to help Shane put the second pad over the abdominal wound.

"Nate, come here and hold pressure," she instructed. "I want to be sure that he still has a pulse."

Nate took over holding pressure on the shoulder wound and she found Creighton's pulse. His heart was fast and thready. He needed volume, fluids and blood. She could easily imagine the damage the bullets had done.

"I'm so glad you found me," she murmured to Shane. "I was doing my best to stall, giving you time to get here."

A muscle ticked in the corner of his mouth. "You did a good job," he said with admiration in his tone. "But if anything had happened to you—"

"But it didn't," she said quickly. "I'm safe and I have you to thank for that, and so much more."

Shane stared at her and she could tell from the raw emotion glimmering there that he was still torn up at how close she'd come to being hurt. More than anything, she wanted to throw herself into his arms, telling him everything would be okay.

Even though she wasn't sure that was true, especially after the painful memories that had come rushing back.

"Shane, I—"

"I hear sirens," Nate said, interrupting them. "The paramedics will be here shortly."

Gabby nodded, keeping her fingers pressed against Creighton's pulse, knowing she'd need to do CPR soon if the paramedic team didn't hurry.

A few minutes later the crew arrived, quickly getting to work inserting an IV and providing life-saving fluids. Once they had Creighton connected to the heart monitor and the fluids running, they picked him up and set him on the gurney.

The three of them moved back, giving the paramedic team room to get Creighton out of there.

"Make sure someone goes with him," Shane directed to Nate.

"Will do."

"We need to wash up," she said, heading into the kitchen. Shane followed, and as soon as they were finished cleaning up, she turned to face him.

"I know where they are," she said with a sigh.

He frowned. "What, you mean the account numbers?"

She nodded slowly, hating the fact that her father had started this more than two decades ago. Had gotten greedy and taken money that hadn't belonged to him.

The pounding headache was gone, replaced by heartbreaking sorrow. So much loss...and for what? Money that her father hadn't even been able to use.

Her father may have started this, but she intended to end it.

Once and for all.

SEVENTEEN

Shane stared at Gabby, watching the myriad of emotions that flitted across her face.

Regret. Sadness. Grim resolve.

He wanted to pick up their conversation where she'd left off, but this wasn't the time. He'd heard her conversation with Creighton and they needed to find out the truth.

"Where are the account numbers, Gabby?" he asked gently. He ached to hold her in his arms but forced himself to give her room. Those minutes that she'd been gone were the longest he'd ever been forced to endure. Worse than being on the run while undercover. He wanted to hug her for himself, but she deserved space. She looked so fragile, so lost.

"Tell me," he said encouragingly. "Where are they?"

Her expression was weary as she turned her face up to his. "I remembered everything," she said in a quavering voice. "You were right, as soon as I faced my memories, the headaches disappeared. I remembered what happened to my father, because I was there. I was hiding beneath my father's desk when they killed him. And when they threw him to the floor, I could see his battered, swollen face against the carpet."

The stark sorrow on her face was more than he could bear. Despite his earlier resolve, he moved closer and carefully drew her into his arms. He kept his embrace comforting as he tucked her head beneath his chin.

"I'm sorry, Gabby," he murmured against her hair. "No child should have to see that. I'm so sorry for everything you've been through."

She relaxed against him, wrapping her arms around his waist and holding on tight. "I didn't want to believe my father was a criminal," she said in a muffled voice. "After my mother married Richard, I built my father up in my mind, telling myself how wonderful our lives would be if he were still alive. But I was wrong. My father was a criminal who died for nothing more than greed."

Shane's heart squeezed in his chest, wishing there was something he could say to make her feel better.

"Subconsciously, I became a trauma surgeon, dedicated my life to helping those who were beaten or shot because of that day I listened to my father being murdered."

"I'm sorry," Shane whispered again. "But think about all the people you saved, Gabby. So many lives that you've touched."

But she was still shaking her head, as if she hadn't heard. "And you know what's even worse?" she asked, meeting his gaze. "I took his name back…that's how Creighton found me. He saw that news story about the airport shooting and came after me."

"Because he thought you still had the money," he said, picking up the thread of her thoughts. "But you had no idea what he was even looking for, did you?"

She shook her head. "Not until he slipped about the account numbers."

He rubbed her back, trying to offer comfort.

"Guess my family genes aren't the greatest," she said with a weary sigh.

"You're not alone, Gabby," he said. "My dad was a great cop who died in the line of duty, but my mother had problems. After my dad died, I went a little crazy, getting into trouble, breaking the law. I got caught but was lucky the judge took pity on me, sending me to a school for troubled teens."

She looked surprised by the revelation. "Really?"

"Yep." He needed to tell her everything to help make his point. "I met Isaac there, you remember Leah's husband, right?" when she nodded, he continued, "We both managed to turn our lives around, becoming cops who uphold the law rather than break it. But my mother spiraled downhill after my father passed away. She literally drank herself to death, and died while Leah was in nursing school."

Gabby's eyes filled with compassion. "Oh, Shane, I'm so sorry to hear that."

"Thanks, but this just proves how much we have in common," he continued huskily. "Our parents made mistakes, we both also made mistakes. But what counts the most are the decisions we made to turn our lives around. I chose law enforcement and you chose being a surgeon. Both admirable professions. It doesn't matter where we came from, it only matters where we're going. And knowing that God will help guide us."

Her expression softened and she slowly nodded. "You're right, Shane. What's in the past doesn't matter as long as we learn from it and move forward from here."

"Exactly," he murmured, aching with the need to kiss her.

But the moment was gone in a heartbeat. Gabby stepped away from him, straightening her shoulders. "Okay, we need to go back to the motel, to pick up my things. I'll show you where the information is."

Shane frowned, then remembered what she

meant. "Your cedar box? But surely you would have known if the account numbers were in there."

For the first time since he'd rescued her from Creighton, the barest hint of a smile tugged at the corner of her mouth. "I believe they're hidden inside my mother's charm bracelet. Remember the way she kept talking about the circus and the drum? There's a drum on the charm bracelet, the gift my father had given my mother that day of the circus. I think there could be some sort of microchip hidden inside."

"Incredible," he muttered. "A microchip. Who would have thought?"

Gabby sighed. "If I had faced my nightmares earlier, maybe I would have figured this out sooner. I'm sorry, Shane. I'm so sorry I put you and your team in danger."

"Remember what I told you right from the very beginning? This is Creighton's fault, not yours. No one's perfect, Gabby. We've all made mistakes."

"This was a whopper," she said with a frown. "But as you said, we'll move forward from here. Let's go. The sooner I get rid of that microchip, the better. I'm more than ready to put all of this behind me."

She brushed past him, apparently in a hurry to get out of Richard's house.

Shane's gut wrenched painfully as he followed Gabby outside. This was it, the end of the case.

He didn't need to spend all his time with Gabby, since she no longer needed his protection.

And Gabby was already pulling away, putting distance between them.

Whatever feelings she may have had for him would soon fade away, just the way his fiancée's had.

But his wouldn't. His chest was so tight he could barely breathe. He loved her. More than he could have ever imagined possible. Completely different than what he'd felt for Linda.

Yet the kindest thing he could do for Gabby at this point was to let her go.

Even though he knew she'd take his heart with her.

Gabby sat beside Shane as he drove Nate's police-issue SUV back to the motel. Tears kept pricking her eyes and she tried to subtly wipe them away.

Ridiculous to miss Shane when he wasn't even gone yet. What was wrong with her? Must be the result of overwhelming relief at knowing that she was safe at last.

But the knot in her stomach didn't feel like relief. It felt like abject sorrow. She didn't want Shane to leave, to go back to his life.

Leaving her to return to hers.

She was humbled by what he'd shared with her, and knowing how he'd overcome his past to become a cop only made her admire him more. She cared about him so much, but he didn't believe her feelings were real.

But she knew they were. Very real. She swallowed hard and fought back her tears, turning to stare out the passenger-side window. Protruding over the tops of the red, gold, orange and green leaves on the trees, she could see the tip of the church steeple where she and Shane had attended services. She took a moment to shake off her melancholy mood and thanked God for saving them. Every one of them.

Shane, Nate and Jenna had all come to her rescue. Plus other deputies that she didn't know by name.

Nate's phone rang, interrupting her thoughts. When he mentioned something about the FBI, she turned in her seat to look at him in surprise.

Nate disconnected from the call. "The FBI is sending two agents out to meet us at the motel. Guess they want that microchip very badly."

"FBI?" Shane echoed with a frown. "When did Griff get in touch with the feds?"

"Not sure, but we shouldn't be surprised. Execution-style shootings reek of mob influence."

"Yeah, I know. At least they stayed out of our way this time," Shane said. He reached over to give Gabby's hand a squeeze. "Don't worry, you'll be fine."

"Thanks," she murmured, knowing he was

right. She *would* be fine, especially with Shane by her side.

The trip to the motel didn't take long. When they arrived, there were several police vehicles already there. She wasn't too surprised to see Griff was waiting, standing beside a tall man and a slender woman both wearing navy blue suits, clearly the FBI agents.

"Dr. Fielding," Griff greeted her formally. "This is Logan Quail and his wife, Kate. They're both special agents with the FBI and have expertise with mafia-related crimes."

She held out her hand. "Nice to meet you, but please call me Gabby."

"Nice to meet y'all," Logan said with a distinct Texas drawl as he shook her hand and then Shane's. The way Logan tugged at the collar of his shirt, she suspected he didn't wear a business suit often.

Once the formalities of introductions were over, Gabby gestured to the motel room she'd stayed in. "If you'll follow me, I'll show you where I think the account numbers are hidden."

Shane stayed close by her side as she entered the motel room and crossed over to where she'd left her cedar box sitting on the dresser. She opened it up, looking down at her personal mementos, without experiencing the crippling pain she used to. After pulling the cedar box out, she set it on the dresser and opened it up. The charm bracelet looked innocent enough, but she knew differently. She picked it up and carefully inspected the charm that was shaped like a drum.

"There's a seam all the way around it," she said, glancing up at the group of people waiting patiently behind her. "I need a knife."

"Here, I'll do it." Shane took out a small penknife and set the drum on the table before inserting the tip of the blade in the seam. With a crack, the drum opened, revealing a small microchip.

"Here you go," Gabby said, gesturing toward it. "I hope you're able to read the technology from twenty-one years ago."

Logan and Kate exchanged a knowing look. "It won't be easy, but we think we have the capability to read it," Kate said.

"Take it. I hope it helps you in some way." Gabby stepped back, glad to be rid of the thing that had caused so much pain and sorrow. She glanced over at Shane. "I'd like to go home."

"I'm sorry, but the crime scene techs are still there," Shane said with obvious regret.

"Then take me to the hospital," she said firmly. "I need to let my boss know that I'm officially off my leave of absence."

Shane nodded and Gabby was a little surprised when no one tried to stop them. Shane walked over to the car he'd borrowed from Nate's aunt, so she slid into the passenger seat.

Neither one of them said much as he drove

toward the freeway. Sneaking a look at his strong, handsome profile, Gabby wanted to ask when she'd see him again. But she feared he'd only tell her again that what she was feeling wasn't real.

"Will someone let me know when I can go back home?" she asked, finally breaking the silence.

Shane glanced at her and nodded. "Yes, I'll make sure of that."

Would he be the one to follow up with her? Or was that just wishful thinking on her part? Gabby racked her brain, trying to think of a way to convince Shane that her feelings weren't just gratitude. But love.

Real, heart-wrenching love.

When he pulled up in front of the hospital, she paused for a moment, turning to face him. "Thanks again, Shane, for saving my life."

His smile seemed sad. "You saved mine first, remember?"

She nodded, knowing she'd never forget. Gabby leaned over to press a kiss against his cheek. "Take care of yourself," she murmured, blinking back tears. She ducked her head, opened the passenger-side door and quickly got out of the car before she could beg him to let her stay with him.

Forever.

The moment she stepped inside the hospital,

she was greeted by the familiar scent of antiseptic. She looked around, a little surprised to realize that things felt different.

Shaking off the sensation, she decided to look in on Brandon Johnson, her colleague who'd been attacked by Creighton.

But when she inquired about where Brandon was, she discovered he'd been discharged home. Which was good news, even though she wished she'd had a chance to apologize.

With nothing else to do, she went to check in with her boss, Jonathan Murray.

"Glad to have you back, Gabby," Jonathan said. "We're running a bit shorthanded, so if you want to pitch in and take second call tonight, I'd appreciate it."

"Sure thing," she said, forcing a smile. Second call also meant covering the ICU patients, so after changing into scrubs, she went up to check on the trauma patients there.

Joe Chasco was still a patient in the ICU, although things didn't look good. His brain wasn't functioning well and she knew that even if Joe survived, he'd never go back to being a surgeon.

She worked with the residents, making rounds and getting up to speed on what medical care was needed, but for some reason, everything felt off. Normally, work consumed her, making her feel as if she belonged.

But not today. A reaction from everything that had transpired? Maybe. But she didn't think so.

Before she met Shane, she'd used work as a way to avoid her personal feelings. Maybe to make up for her father's death. But Shane had exposed her to faith and church and so much more.

Love. She loved him so much, she ached with it.

And suddenly, she knew exactly how she could convince him to give the feelings between them a chance.

Shane finished up what seemed like a mountain of paperwork related to everything that had transpired with Creighton. But his mind kept wandering back to Gabby.

He must have picked up the phone a dozen times, intending to call her at the hospital. Just to hear her voice. But he forced himself to wait until Griff had informed him that the crime scene techs had finally finished at her house.

"Good, that's good," he muttered, suddenly nervous about calling Gabby now. The time wasn't too late, just seven-thirty at night, but dusk had fallen and he wondered if it would be better to let it go until the morning.

But the thought of Gabby spending another night in one of those tiny call rooms convinced him to at least offer her the choice. He took a deep breath and made the call to the hospital, asking for her to be paged.

He was on hold for less than a minute before she responded, "This is Gabby Fielding, may I help you?"

Shane swallowed hard, suddenly nervous. "Hi, Gabby, it's me, Shane. I have good news," he added in a rush. "Your house has been cleared. You're free to return home any time."

"Really? That's wonderful," she responded, sounding relieved.

"Well, there might be a bit of a mess," he cautioned. "I'd be happy to give you a hand if you'd like."

"I don't want to be a bother," Gabby said, although he could hear a bit of hesitation in her voice.

"It's not a bother. How about I meet you there?" The offer was more of a knee-jerk reaction, but as soon as he said the words, he knew he meant them.

No way was he leaving Gabby to face her house alone, in the dark.

"Okay, thanks, Shane. See you soon."

He disconnected from the call and jumped up from his desk. Nate lifted his eyebrows when Shane headed past him. "Need help with something?"

Shane paused but then shook his head. "No,

I'm just going to help Gabby clean up the mess the crime scene techs left behind."

Nate smiled wryly and shook his head. "Well, at least she's not a suspect anymore."

There wasn't a good response for that, so he just lifted his hand in a wave and hurried out to his car, his personal SUV since Griff hadn't given him anything to replace the police-issue vehicle Nate had turned in on his behalf.

Staying under the speed limit wasn't easy, although he knew there was no reason to rush. Other than to satisfy the ridiculous need to see Gabby again.

Man, he was in trouble. Big trouble.

Gabby's car was already in the driveway when he arrived and there were lights on in what seemed like every room in the modest house. Apparently she didn't want to be in the dark, even though the danger was over.

He knocked sharply on the front door and then walked inside, sweeping his gaze over the living room. "Gabby? Are you okay?"

"Hi, Shane," she said, coming out from the kitchen. "Are you hungry? There isn't much, but I just threw in a frozen pizza."

"Sounds good." She looked wonderful, her long red curls framing her face, making him wish he could bury his fingers in the lush strands and kiss her as if she belonged to him. But that wasn't why he was here. He followed her into the kitchen, frowning when he realized she was already putting her things back where they belonged.

"You know, there's no rush. You don't have to do all this tonight," he told her. "I could give Leah and Isaac a call in the morning, I'm sure they wouldn't mind helping us."

"I know, I just thought that I should try to get back to my normal routine," she said with a sigh. "But even being at work didn't seem normal."

"It may take a while, Gabby," he said gently, deeply concerned about her well-being. "You might want to take some time off work, maybe talk to someone."

She frowned and shrugged. "Maybe, but in some ways, I'm glad to be able to put some of the past to rest. It's just—everything seems different now."

"Like what?" He sank into the chair beside her and took her hands in his. "Talk to me."

She took a deep breath before looking him directly in the eye. "I've fallen in love with you, Shane."

His heart thudded with joy, but then he forced himself to face the truth. "We talked about this, Gabby. You're grateful to be alive, and frankly, I'm glad you're alive, too. But in a few days, maybe even weeks, this feeling will pass."

But she was already shaking her head. "No, it

won't. I know my own feelings, Shane. I'm not your former fiancée."

He wanted so badly to believe her. "I care about you, too, Gabby."

"You believe in God, in faith, right?"

"Yes." He stared at her, trying to follow her logic.

"I only went to church once, but I instantly felt a sense of peace. I can't see faith, or hold it in my hand, but I know it's there. I'm asking you to do the same with me. To believe in my love for you. To believe that I know the difference between gratitude and love." Her voice broke and she swallowed hard before continuing. "I understand you might not feel the same way, but I need you to know what's in my heart."

And suddenly he understood. How could he have been so stupid? "You're right, Gabby. I've known that I was in love with you for a while now but refused to believe you felt the same way. Because I was too afraid of being hurt the way I was in the past. But that was wrong. I shouldn't have assumed you'd be like Linda, when you're nothing like her."

"Really? You love me?" she asked breathlessly.

He laughed, leaping to his feet and sweeping her into his arms. "Yes, I love you, Gabriella Fielding. More than I can possibly say."

When he set her down, she wrapped her arms around his neck and gazed up at him, her beautiful green eyes bright with unshed tears. "I'm so glad. Because I can't imagine what my life would be like without you."

He kissed her tenderly, knowing they were totally in sync because he felt exactly the same way.

EPILOGUE

Gabby left the hospital, exhausted from her long shift yet excited to be having dinner with Shane. For the past couple of months they'd spent every moment of their free time together, growing closer than she'd ever thought possible.

Granted there had been dark times where she'd struggled with putting everything behind her. She'd spoken to Kristin, the sheriff's department psychologist to help come to grips with the fact that her father had been a criminal. And she'd wrestled with guilt after Joe Chasco had died. But being with Shane and attending church had helped her find peace and joy.

She'd never been this happy. It was as if every day was a new gift. And she'd been humbled and pleased when Shane's sister, Leah, and her husband, Isaac, had welcomed her into their family with open arms.

Today was her birthday, and even though she'd never told Shane about it, he'd asked her to come to his house for dinner. She wasn't expecting anything special; after all, they'd pretty much taken turns making dinner on their days off.

She'd actually been pleasantly surprised to discover Shane was a decent cook. Probably better than she was.

The chill in the air made her shiver and she hurried to her car. As she drove to Shane's, she enjoyed seeing the Christmas lights decorating several of the houses along the way.

She pulled into his driveway and shut off the engine, smiling when she noticed he was waiting for her in the doorway.

"You're right on time," he said, after giving her a big hug and kiss.

"Aren't I always?" she teased.

"No," he said honestly. "But it's not your fault when your patients don't cooperate."

"Something smells good," she murmured, sniffing the air. "Did you make a pumpkin pie? Thanksgiving is over, you know."

"Isn't pumpkin pie your favorite?" Shane asked, as he helped her with her coat.

"Yes," she acknowledged with a smile. "But you prefer pecan pie."

"Who's to say we don't have both?" he asked. He tossed her coat over the back of the chair. "Have a seat on the sofa."

"Okay," she said, even though she thought his

request was a little odd. She patted the seat beside her. "How was your day?"

Instead of sitting beside her, he dropped to his knees. And when he pulled out a small velvet box, she gasped.

"Gabriella, I want you to know how much I love you. From the moment you saved my life, I couldn't get you out of my mind. And ever since that moment, I've only grown more in love with you. I know this might seem a little fast, but will you please marry me?"

Tears of joy sprang to her eyes and she nodded eagerly. "Yes, Shane, of course I'll marry you!" Ignoring the box, she leaned over to hug him. They clung together for several long moments before she lifted her head to look up at him. "Shane, you're everything I've ever wanted in a husband. You've shown me the power of faith and love and I'm the luckiest woman in the world to have you." She swallowed hard and swiped away her tears. "Your proposal is doubly precious. You probably don't realize it, but today is my birthday."

"I knew," he said, drawing her up to her feet. He kissed her, but before she could deepen the kiss, he lifted his head. Dazed, she jumped when she suddenly heard a loud "Surprise!"

People poured into the living room holding balloons and streamers and a huge birthday cake.

"How did you know?" she asked as Shane took

the diamond engagement ring out and slipped it on her ring finger.

"He looked it up on your driver's license," Nate said, grinning broadly. "Congrats!"

She pulled Shane's head down for another kiss, before turning to greet the rest of their guests.

Apparently, life with Shane would never be dull. And surrounded by friends and family, she knew she belonged here with Shane. Home at last.

* * * * *

Dear Reader,

Thank you so much for the wonderful emails and letters that you've sent regarding my SWAT: Top Cops—Love in the line of duty series. In the third book, *Under the Lawman's Protection*, you met Leah's brother, Shane Hawkins, who was working as an undercover police officer. You also briefly met Dr. Gabriella Fielding, the trauma surgeon who came out to the cabin to help save Shane's life.

Forgotten Memories is Shane and Gabby's story. When Shane witnesses Gabby being abducted from outside the hospital parking lot, he doesn't hesitate to risk his life in a daring attempt to save her. Gabby is willing to do her part, although she's grateful for Shane's assistance. As they try to find the key to unlock Gabby's buried memories, both Shane and Gabby find a greater treasure: love.

I hope you enjoy Shane and Gabby's story. I very much enjoy hearing from my readers. If you're interested in dropping me a brief note or signing up for my newsletter, please visit my website at laurascottbooks.com. I'm also on Facebook at Laura Scott Books Author and on Twitter @Laurascottbooks.

Yours in faith,
Laura Scott

LARGER-PRINT BOOKS!

**GET 2 FREE
LARGER-PRINT NOVELS
PLUS 2 FREE
MYSTERY GIFTS**

Love Inspired®

Larger-print novels are now available...

LILP15

REQUEST YOUR FREE BOOKS!
2 FREE WHOLESOME ROMANCE NOVELS IN LARGER PRINT
PLUS 2
FREE
MYSTERY GIFTS

HEARTWARMING™

Wholesome, tender romances

YES! Please send me 2 FREE Harlequin® Heartwarming Larger-Print novels and my 2 FREE mystery gifts (gifts worth about $10). After receiving them, if I don't wish to receive any more books, I can return the shipping statement marked "cancel." If I don't cancel, I will receive 4 brand-new larger-print novels every month and be billed just $5.24 per book in the U.S. or $5.99 per book in Canada. That's a savings of at least 19% off the cover price. It's quite a bargain! Shipping and handling is just 50¢ per book in the U.S. and 75¢ per book in Canada.* I understand that accepting the 2 free books and gifts places me under no obligation to buy anything. I can always return a shipment and cancel at any time. Even if I never buy another book, the two free books and gifts are mine to keep forever.

161/361 IDN GHX2

Name _____ (PLEASE PRINT)

Address _____ Apt. #

City _____ State/Prov. _____ Zip/Postal Code

Signature (if under 18, a parent or guardian must sign)

Mail to the **Reader Service:**
IN U.S.A.: P.O. Box 1867, Buffalo, NY 14240-1867
IN CANADA: P.O. Box 609, Fort Erie, Ontario L2A 5X3

* Terms and prices subject to change without notice. Prices do not include applicable taxes. Sales tax applicable in N.Y. Canadian residents will be charged applicable taxes. Offer not valid in Quebec. This offer is limited to one order per household. Not valid for current subscribers to Harlequin Heartwarming larger-print books. All orders subject to credit approval. Credit or debit balances in a customer's account(s) may be offset by any other outstanding balance owed by or to the customer. Please allow 4 to 6 weeks for delivery. Offer available while quantities last.

Your Privacy—The Reader Service is committed to protecting your privacy. Our Privacy Policy is available online at www.ReaderService.com or upon request from the Reader Service.

We make a portion of our mailing list available to reputable third parties that offer products we believe may interest you. If you prefer that we not exchange your name with third parties, or if you wish to clarify or modify your communication preferences, please visit us at www.ReaderService.com/consumerschoice or write to us at Reader Service Preference Service, P.O. Box 9062, Buffalo, NY 14240-9062. Include your complete name and address.

HW15